Sergeant at War: Letters Home from Vietnam

by Brett Gordon

© Copyright 2025 Brett Gordon

ISBN 979-8-88824-590-3

All rights reserved. No part of this publication may be reproduced, stored in a retrieval system, or transmitted in any form or by any means—electronic, mechanical, photocopy, recording, or any other—except for brief quotations in printed reviews, without the prior written permission of the author.

Published by

◤köehlerbooks™

3705 Shore Drive
Virginia Beach, VA 23455
800-435-4811
www.koehlerbooks.com

SERGEANT AT WAR

SERGEANT AT WAR

Letters Home from Vietnam

BRETT GORDON

VIRGINIA BEACH
CAPE CHARLES

FOREWORD

In August 1965, the 7th Marine Regiment participated in Operation Starlite, also called the Battle of Van Tuong. It was the first major battle against the Vietcong for American troops in South Vietnam. In that same month, my dad, Michael J. Gordon, a twenty-year-old from Sacramento, California, enlisted in the United States Marine Corps. After boot camp, he shipped off to Vietnam where he quickly learned the horrors of war, while also rising through the ranks to staff sergeant.

Like many war veterans, my dad rarely talked about his time in the military or in Vietnam, and he never went back to see the land where so much blood was shed. So, it was a revelation to read how he really felt about his military service from recounted letters he'd written to his own father, my grandfather John Gordon, and other family members.

The letters had been stored in an old gun safe, along with a rifle, several handguns, medals, and an inert hand grenade he'd taken from a Viet Cong fighter he had killed. The letters were from my father to his father, starting from boot camp to the day he mustered out. Sadly, that relationship between father and son, while seemingly strong in the letters, became estranged in later years.

I gained tremendous insight into my dad as a young, idealistic man, the greater Vietnam War, and how it affected one of the thousands of young men of his generation. My dad fought with equal fervor for his platoon and his country, ultimately reenlisting after his first tour because he felt that some of the leadership in the field were unable to safeguard the young men under them. Dad believed he could do a better job and save lives. So, he put himself in harm's way again for another two years.

Dad's letters mix the mundane with the profound. *Rainstorms* mean a *bath*. A guy who "looked like a rat" sat on a landmine leaving little left to send home.

Sergeant at War: Letters Home from Vietnam places the reader in a world and war many would like to forget. The Vietnam War has been invoked as a cautionary tale for every US military operation since the war ended in 1975. The estimate of the number of lives lost on both sides ranges from 800,000 to more than three million, civilians and soldiers, not counting the many thousands more injured or missing in action. North and South Vietnam ultimately reunited as one country with a Communist government. Today it is considered a developing country with high levels of poverty, corruption, censorship, and an environment still ravaged by the effects of the war.

My dad's letters home give one soldier's view of the Vietnam War, fought nearly fifty years ago. They're as fresh today as they were in the 1960s. From the first letter to the last, you're so deeply immersed in his world that you feel as though you're listening to him tell his stories—stories you won't forget.

All letters are as my dad wrote them. All wording, spelling, and punctuation are original. Where appropriate typos were corrected, and additional explanatory information is contained in footnotes.

1965

US involvement in the war in Vietnam ramped up significantly in early 1965 when North Vietnamese forces invade South Vietnam. A US helicopter base in the central highlands of South Vietnam was attacked in January, and nine Americans were killed and more than seventy wounded.

On August 17th, the 7th Marine Regiment participated in Operation Starlite, the first major battle against the North Vietnamese for American troops in South Vietnam. President Lyndon Johnson raised America's combat strength in Vietnam to more than sixty thousand troops.

On August 25th, Michael J. Gordon enlisted in the United States Marine Corp (USMC).

BOOT CAMP—SEPTEMBER 5TH, 1965

Dear Dad & Mom,

I have been marching, saluting and saying 'yes sir' until I'm hoarse. Every morning we get up at 5:00 am and go to bed at 9:00 pm. Things aren't really that tough, but I think that is because we have a good Drill Instructor. From what he tells us, things from here on out are going to get rough. I told you we graduate on the 21st of October. From here I will go to Camp Pendleton for about a month. I do not know if I get any leave in-between.

Love Mike

BOOT CAMP—SEPTEMBER 12TH, 1965

Dear Mom & Dad,

I just finished taking an I.Q. test and they told me I did pretty good. I sure hope it's enough to get me to flight school. I also just finished a physical fitness test and they told me that I did pretty good at that too. Right now we are learning about the M-14 rifle. It is a new rifle that will be used by all of our allies. It is a pretty sharp weapon and it replaces all of the old rifles and machine guns. Things aren't really as easy as that last letter must have implied. In fact, they're pretty rough, but it's all for our own good.

With love,
Mike

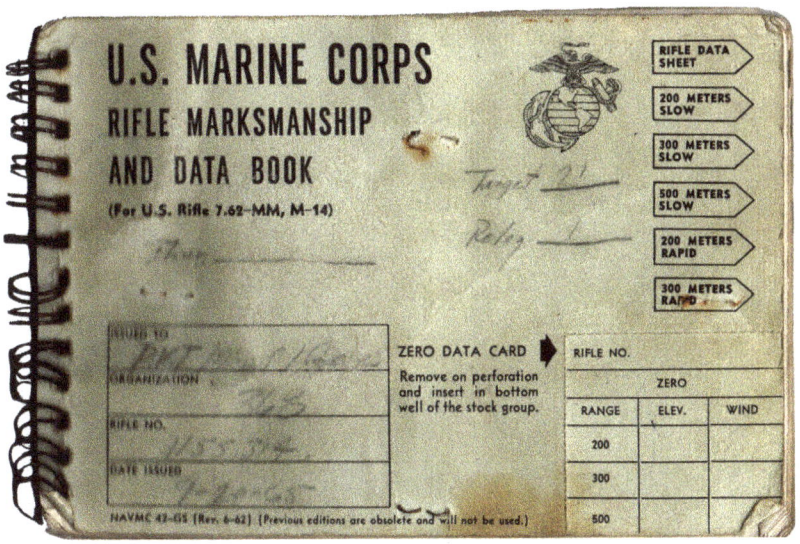

Michael's rifle marksmanship book from his time in boot camp.

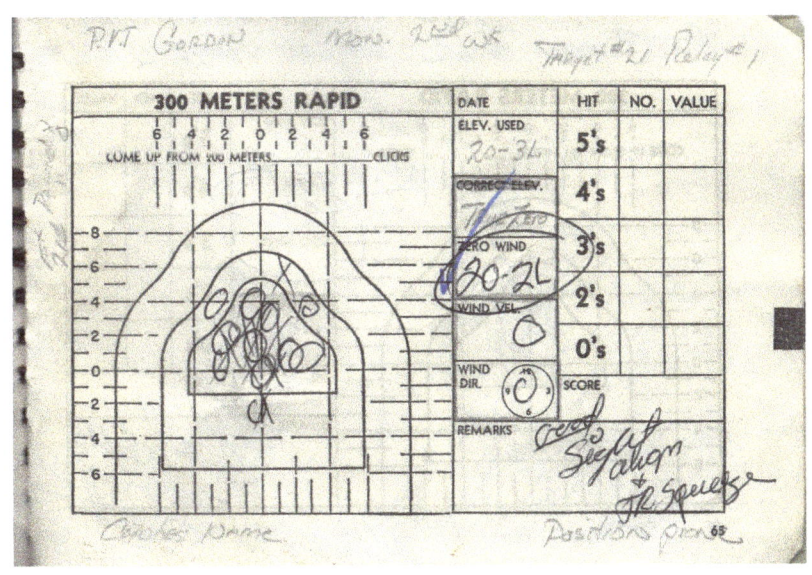

Michael's 300 Meter—Week 2 of boot camp.

BOOT CAMP—SEPTEMBER 19TH, 1965

Dear Mom & Dad,

I would appreciate it if somebody would get Judi Diea's address and mail it to me! I have been attending Morman services on Sunday with a buddy of mine. Sue wrote to me and said Judi was going to be married. I just want to write to her and send my congratulations. I just took another I.Q test and scored in the 90%. I was hoping for a little higher, but it's still really good. My chances are also looking pretty good for pilot school. I received your letter and it was nice to hear from home. If I was to tell you I'm not home sick, I would be lying.

All the time I was away from home I guess I was really still there. On the 17th we go to Camp Pendleton for Rifle practice. I am a squad leader right now and I hope I can keep it up because they are the ones that usually make Private 1st Class out of boot camp. I will not get any leave on the 21st of October, but I should be home somewhere around the 16th of November. Have to go now.

With all my love,
Mike

BOOT CAMP: SEPTEMBER 20TH, 1965

Dear Mom & Dad,

I am writing to you from my barracks. Things are going fine. I will graduate on the 21st of October. I hope everything at home is going fine also. I would like one of you to phone Sue Kershaw and tell her when I am coming home and that everything is fine. You can find her phone number by calling information. Everyday seems like 4 and I can't wait to come home.

With all my love,
Mike

P.S. I am sure glad I had a Marine for a father!

BOOT CAMP—SEPTEMBER 26TH, 1965

Dear Mom and Dad,

Sorry I haven't written lately but things have been getting pretty rushed around here. I only have 26 more days left in boot camp. I am in my second week at the rifle range. I can't remember if I told you but I have been promoted to guide of the platoon. I am almost a sure thing for P.F.C.

I hope everything is going fine at home and everyone is in good health. I don't know if you have seen Sue lately, but she has found an apartment and likes it very much. Sorry I had planned on writing more but I have to go!

Love Mike

BOOT CAMP—OCTOBER 10TH, 1965

Dear Mom & Dad,

I'm sorry I haven't been writing so often but things are starting to get a little rough around here and writing time is a little short!

 I'm still the guide of the platoon and I'm also up for honor man. If I stay as the guide and make honor man, I will be the only one in the platoon to graduate in dress blues. It will also help me to get into flight training school. Today is Sunday October 10th and I just came back from Church. A lot of the fellows are talking about graduation and having their folks attend the ceremonies. I wish both of you could be here, but it is an awfully long way to come for only a few hours, but if for some chance you could make it, that would be the highlight of my graduation. We only have eleven days left counting graduation day and right now that sure sounds good. There has been talk that we are going to be cut shorter as far as boot camp goes but there is no official word. So I may be seeing you sooner than expected. I hope that everything is going all right at home and that everyone is in good health.

Love Mike

P.S. I will phone you on graduation!

BOOT CAMP—OCTOBER 16TH, 1965

Dear Mom & Dad,

Graduation is October 21st and all visitors must be here by 9:30 am in the morning. I am pretty sure I am going to be the one graduating in dress blues, but nothing official. It is a sure thing on P.F.C., so at least I made it that far. I was so glad when I found out that at least one of you would be here for graduation. I think I might be able to phone again Sunday but I don't know what time. I just won $16 on the World Series games and that's quite a lot here.[1]

Sorry I have to cut it short, but time is running out.

Love Mike

---

1 The 1965 World Series was the 62nd edition of the World Series that matched the Los Angeles Dodgers against the Minnesota Twins. The Dodgers beat the Twins, four games to three.

Michael at his graduation from boot camp, October 21, 1965.

Michael Gordon and his platoon. Michael is in the first row on the bottom right.

I am pleased to inform you that your son, Private First Class Michael J. Gordon 2158672, U. S. Marine Corps has been chosen to receive a Dress Blue Uniform awarded by LEATHERNECK Magazine to the outstanding recruit in the platoon.

In order that you may have a complete understanding of Private First Class GORDON's accomplishment, it should be noted that he won h this coveted award in competition with 68 men, all of whom entered the Marine Corps and progressed through training with him. From that number and on the recommendations of his drill instructors, the Marine in the professional platoon who displayed the highest order of skill and professional

knowledge in a wide range of basic military subjects was closely examined. After considering the knowledge, conduct, attitude, military bearing, and leadership potential of all the candidates, your son was judged most worthy to receive the Marine Corps Dress Blue Uniform.

We in the Marine Corps are intensely proud of our Dress Blue Uniform and it is the judgement f those who most closely observed Private First Class GORDON here that he will wear it with distinction to the honor of the

Corps. We are indeed proud to have a young man of such high caliber in our anks, and I know his outstanding performance will be a source of great satisfacti n to you.

INFANTRY TRAINING REGIMENT—OCTOBER 30TH, 1965

Dear Mom & Dad,

I am now at Camp Pendleton and it is not all that it was said to be! Instead of 4 weeks of I.T.R.[2] it may turn into 6 weeks. As of now I don't know exactly when I will be arriving home. One good thing about it is that if it's six weeks long, that means I will be home for X-mas and New Years. I am a guide of a platoon at I.T.R. and maybe if I am lucky I will be coming home as a Lance Corporal. Most of the time here we will be crawling on our stomachs and running through warfare tactics.

I was so proud when I saw Dad standing there talking to the Captain and I was all dressed up in my blues. Having my father attend my graduation made it everything it should have been! I only wish both of my parents could have been there. Sue may be coming by to see the pictures that Dad took of graduation.

Got to go!

All my love,
Mike

---

2   During the Vietnam War era, Marines received training in the Infantry Training Regiment (ITR) that focused on a variety of skills essential for combat in the jungle environment of Vietnam.

INFANTRY TRAINING REGIMENT—NOVEMBER 2ND, 1965

Dear Mom and Dad,

I'm now in my first week of I.T.R. and I've been appointed Company Guide! Everything has been pretty easy so far, but Monday we will go into the field and things will start to get a little rough! I'm now in charge of a whole company instead of a platoon and the responsibility is piling up. I will be here for at least four weeks and maybe I will be transferred to another camp for two more weeks of advanced training! I really don't plan on being home till the 16th of December, give it one day or the other!

I hope those pictures came out alright and I'm awaiting the day till I can look at them myself. I still don't know whether I'm going to be accepted for O.C.S.[3] or whether I'm going to Vietnam, but either way I'm going to try my best!

I hope everything is going alright at home and that everyone is still in good health. Now to answer some of your questions from your letter; Camp Pendleton is 40 miles south of San Diego. Tom Knoble is in a Tank Battalion and I haven't seen him since I arrived at camp. Steve is still in the hospital. I'm sure Steve will be out pretty soon, but he will have to return to San Diego to complete boot camp. Tom will only be at Camp Pendleton for two weeks and then he'll probably be home for his twenty day leave.

Well, I've got to go so give my love to everyone and tell them I'll see them soon. I miss both of you very much!

Love Mike

---

3   O.C.S., the Marine Corps Officer Candidates School, is a training course designed to screen and evaluate potential Marine Corps officers.

INFANTRY TRAINING REGIMENT—NOVEMBER 14TH, 1965

Dear Mom and Dad,

Sorry I haven't written as often as I should, but things have been pretty hectic around here. We have gone through all kinds of training and fired just about every weapon the Marine Corp has to offer. As everything looks now, I will be home around the 16th of December and it will be for a 20 day leave. I'm still in charge of a company of men and everything is going fine. I still don't know whether or not I will be going to O.C.S., but in a few days I should be taking some more tests to see if I am qualified. If I do qualify, I might have to stay here for a while longer, which means I might not be home when I planned.

When I do get out of here, I should get around $150.00, so at least I won't be broke when I get home. All the time I've been training in the Corp I've been saving money out of my pay by no choice of my own.

So, as you can see, they're not paying us much each month and if you just happen to have that $25 you were going to give me before I left I could sure use it.

I never realized how much I would like military life until last weekend when I had shore liberty and actually got a look at civilian life again. We have it pretty good and I'm sure glad I'm a Marine. I've got to go, give all my love to everyone!

Love Mike
Hope to see you soon!

ADVANCED TRAINING —DECEMBER 10TH, 1965

Dear Mom and Dad,

How's everything at home! I don't believe I am going to make it into flight school so I guess I'll have to go into some other field. Right now I'm in training to be a specialized combat marine. I will be home on the 17th of December. The days are starting to drag along and I can hardly wait to get home. I heard that Gary was living with Dave and Larry?

I weigh 200lbs now and I think I've changed in more ways than one. I graduated out of I.T.R. and so far out of boot camp and I.T.R. I've gotten 4.8 conduct and pro marks. A 5.0 is as high as you can get. Lights are going out so I can't say as much as I would like to.

I love you both!
Mike

1966

1966 marked an increase in the number of US troops on the ground. By the end of the year American forces numbered 385,000, plus sixty thousand more sailors offshore. The year began with Operation Crimp, involving nearly eight thousand troops in an effort to capture Vietcong headquarters in Chu Chi in northwest Vietnam. On August 3, the US launched Operation Prairie. Marines conducted reconnaissance patrols in northern Quang Tri Province. Marine infantry, reinforced by tanks, artillery, and air support, engaged the North Vietnamese in heavy fighting.

DEPLOYMENT—JANUARY 18TH, 1966

Well I'm now in Hawaii as you can see by the postcard. I'm sorry I couldn't talk to you longer on the phone. I'll be in Okinawa for about 6 weeks and then onto Vietnam.

I'm still trying my best.

Love you both,
Mike

DEPLOYMENT—JANUARY 19TH, 1966

My address is PFC Michael J Gordon 2158672

F. Co. 2nd BN F.M.F 5th Marines

F.P.O San Francisco, California

I'll be home about Feb. or Mar. of "67". Hope to be a little higher in grade.

I miss you and love you both,
Mike

DEPLOYMENT—JANUARY 19TH, 1966

Dear Mom and Dad,

Couldn't say much on a Postcard so I am writing a short letter. Today is my second day in Hawaii and I will be shipping out tomorrow morning. I'll be six weeks in Okinawa and six months in Vietnam, then the rest of my tour will probably be in Japan. I have about 20 more days aboard the ship before I hit Okinawa. I'm going to try to take pictures while I am overseas so I'll probably be sending them home. I hope to make E-3 my March or April at the latest. I'm trying my best and things look pretty good. If I can make E-4 by the time I hit the states or a little after, I'll be able to request some type of school. Although they say I'll have to serve another tour of duty in Vietnam. Most of the guys that I am going over with now are in their second tour of duty in Vietnam. I hope that everything is going fine at home and everyone is in good health!

With Love,
Mike

DEPLOYMENT—JANUARY 22ND, 1966

Dear Mom and Dad,

I'm now three days off the Coast of Okinawa. Life aboard ship has been very trying and I'll be glad to get off. This is probably the smallest ship in the Navy and we have about 1,000 men aboard. I'll have a few days of liberty in Okinawa and then onto 6 weeks of training, seven days a week. By March I should be making E-3 and if I'm lucky I might make E-4 before I return to the states.

Things are starting to look up around here so maybe it won't be so bad after all. There's all kinds of talk about what's going to happen to us, but as of yet everything still points to Vietnam. As I said before, I will have to serve another tour of duty overseas before my enlistment is up. I might get out of it if I sign a six month extension on this tour of duty. So I don't know whether I'll be back on February 2nd or not.

How are things at home and do you ever see or hear from Sue? I'll write to you soon again.

Love and miss you both,
Mike

OKINAWA/VIETNAM—FEBRUARY 15TH, 1966

Things are going pretty good over here in Okinawa. They're having a little trouble over there in Vietnam as you have probably already heard. Our company is on call to go in at any time, so I may be there before I'd expected. I'm in a rifle company, which means I should see quite a bit of action. Promotions are coming up March 1st and I hope I make E-3. My chances look pretty good!

The sanitary conditions in the towns over there are pretty filthy and the V.D rate is very high.[4]

The only time most of us leave the base is when we need something that the P.X. doesn't have.

When we do go, we can't go by ourselves because there is a lot a Communist belief in the towns!

Prices are very cheap over here. Beer is 15 cents a bottle and mixed drinks vary from 25 cents to 30 cents. Pure silk suits like the ones I had for $75.00 cost $37.00 tailor made. If there is anything you want just write and tell me and I will send it home.

Time is passing very quickly over here and in no time I should be on a boat headed for home. I hope that everything is going fine at home and that everyone is in good health. Give my love to the Dormarts. I've got to go for now. I send my love to both of you!

Love Mike

---

[4] Venereal diseases (VD), now called sexually transmitted diseases, spread mainly through sexual contact. Common diseases at the time were syphilis, gonorrhea, and chlamydia.

VIETNAM—FEBRUARY 24TH, 1966

Dear Mom and Dad,

I am now at the northern end of South Vietnam. Two days ago our platoon had to rescue a squad that got trapped in a village. They received a few casualties but we came out alright. The Viet Cong weren't so lucky! The climate is very hot and rain doesn't come too often. Our platoon goes out on patrols at night, but we haven't had any more action. I have just been put on mess duty for 15 days, so I won't be going out with them for a while!

The people over here have all kinds of diseases and their teeth are black from eating betel nuts. Betel Nut is a small drug that grows on a small tree and the juice from the nut relieves the pain![5]

None of the people seem to like Americans and there is no way of telling who's your enemy till they shoot!

I've got to go for now. I miss you both

Love Mike

---

5   Betel nut chewing is an important cultural practice in some regions in south and southeast Asia and the Asia Pacific region. It has traditionally played an important role in social customs, religious practices and cultural rituals.

Michael Gordon in his early days in Vietnam. Photo by Lee Suydam.

VIETNAM—MAY 2ND, 1966

Dear Mom and Dad,

I have just returned from a 5 day sweep around Chu Lai and I am now sitting on a perimeter around Chu Lai Marine Corp Air Base. My warrant for E-3 came through April 1st but the raise in pay has yet to catch up with me! It is hard to fight a war not knowing who is your friend and who is your enemy! South Vietnam has A.R.V.N, which are supposed to be the army of Vietnam and the Popular Forces which are villagers that fight Viet Cong.[6,7,8]

Neither one of these groups can be trusted because too many of them turned out to be V.C. The only rule here to determine if they are V.C. is to wait till they shoot! Every time I return from patrol I have the feeling that I have cheated death one more day because we are just sitting ducks in a pond. I do really believe that I'll make it home because it's going to take a lot of V.C. to stop me.

I wrote Sue and told her we are through because I can see no way that I can get married until I get out of the service. Also I have to keep my mind on my job and not somebody five-thousand miles away! I know at one time I thought I loved her, but I can't say that I do anymore. It is funny how people change over here and I know

---

6   ARVN—The Army of the Republic of Vietnam comprised the ground forces of the South Vietnamese military from its inception in 1955 to the fall of Saigon in April 1975.
7   Popular Force (PF)—The South Vietnamese Popular Force was a part-time local militia of the Army of the Republic of Vietnam (ARVN) during the Vietnam War.
8   Vietcong (VC)—The Vietnamese Communists, or Vietcong, were the military branch of the National Liberation Front (NLF) and were commanded by the Central Office for South Vietnam, which was located near the Cambodian border.

I have. When I first came here I felt sorry for these people, but after seeing some of my fellow marines get shot, all of my sorrow and pity left and now hate and contempt for these people is all I have left. I have not turned savage like some marines do, but at times I feel the same way!

All in all I'm really doing fine. I've lost a little weight and I've got a beautiful suntan! Larry wrote and said he was all set for his wedding. I wish I could be there. If you happen to have some extra goodies laying around you might send them my way because they are very hard to come by over here.

I got to close for now. I'll see you in "seven" months.

I love you both.
Love Mike

P.S. Dear Thelda

I have been hoping to be able to get into a village and get you something for Mother's Day, but I am way out here in the sticks. I haven't had a chance. So I'm wishing you a very happy Mother's Day and I send all my love! "Happy Mother's Day."

Love Mike

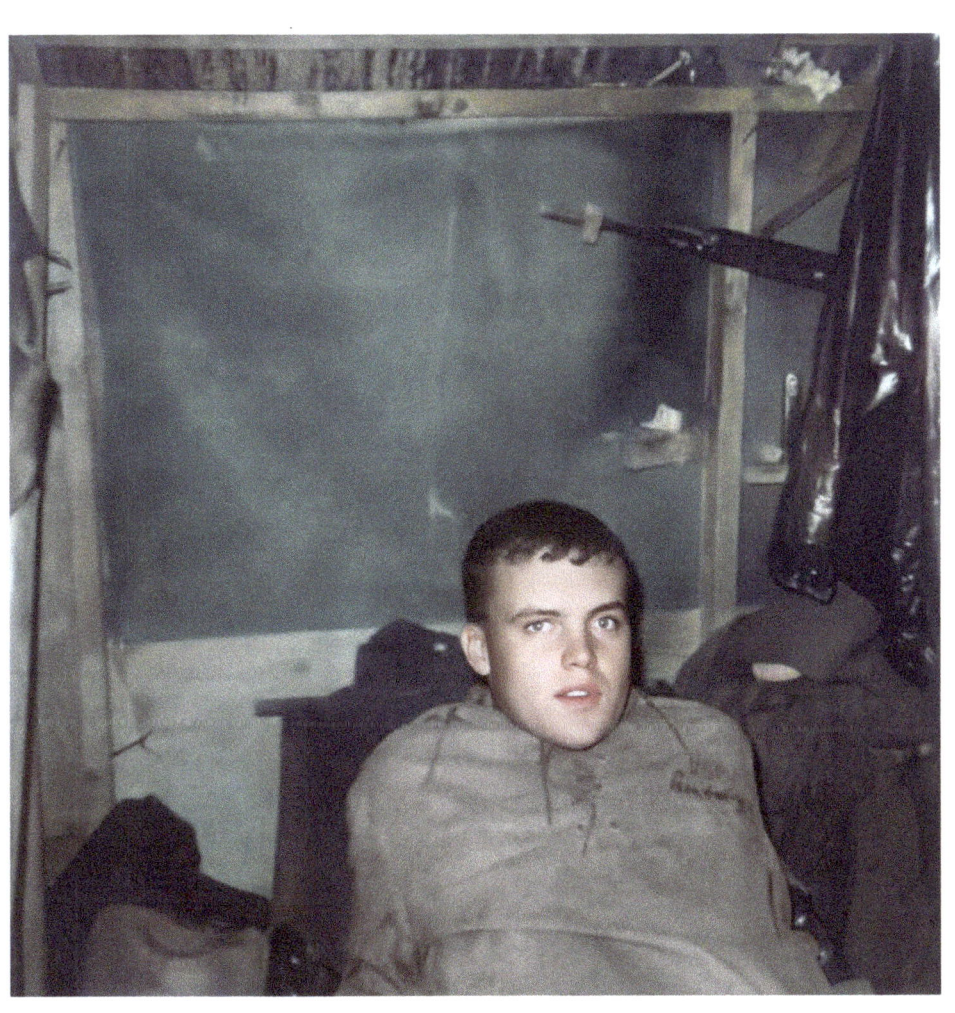

VIETNAM—MAY 16TH, 1966

Dear Dad,

In three days we move from our perimeter back to the Mountain. We have been working on immediate action drills in case we get ambushed or draw sniper fire. I imagine that they have told you over the news that the war isn't going our way. I think the V.C. are finally becoming wise to our tactics. There has been word that Red China has been sending forces to join the V.C., but no definite word. What do the newspapers say about this war coming to an end!

I've heard that the girls back in the states are protesting against sending all men overseas. Reports come in that there are seven girls to every boy. That should be nice when I get back to the states! The Lieutenant just announced that we rate five ribbons so far. It's sure going to be nice to have something on my chest besides that marksman medal. I also hope that by the time I get home I will have Corporal Chevrons in place of Lance Corporal.

Business should start picking up for you with the hot weather coming on shouldn't it? I imagine with working and trying to keep the house up, you just about have your hands full. I hope that everything is working out ok, especially with the wedding and all coming up.

Take it easy and keep smiling, you're a very handsome man when you smile—sometimes you're even better looking than I am! I'm always thinking of you

Love Mike

VIETNAM—MAY 17TH, 1966

I was sorry to hear about Thelda and yourself, but as you have stated it is for the better. It is kind of hard to imagine you as a bachelor, but I'll bet you'll make a darn good one. As I wrote in my last letter, I have called it quits with Sue due to quite a few facts in not being able to trust her!

My warrant for E-3 came through on April 1st and now I am in charge of some men again. I am still on a perimeter around Chu Lai Marine Corps Air Base which is located midway between Chu Lai and Da Nang. I was supposed to be on mess duty for fifteen days, but they pulled me off for the last sweep!

I don't know how long we are going to stay here, but pretty soon we are going to move into V.C. valley. If we do go, we are guaranteed to see some action!

We have lost quite a few people already and even had one crack up and lose his mind. There is quite a bit of strain put on the mind because most of the fighting is done at night! The only time that I got a little shook up was on the last sweep. We had gone all the way without seeing a single V.C. and when evening chow came we became slack and were just sitting in a circle bullshitting.

All of a sudden the dirt around us was being torn up by sniper fire - you never saw three people move so fast! I still don't know how they missed all three of us.

When we came across sniper fire on another night, one of our guys got hit in the foot. When they got around to fixing him up they found powder burns on his boot. He shot himself and tried to say a V.C. shot him!

I never knew it would be like this when people told me what it was like. It's hard to describe how I felt when a Corpsman friend of mine had a bullet enter his right eye and come out the left side of his head. I saw it happen, but at least I knew it was a quick death.

These statements may sound a little harsh, but in every war the same thing happens. I could probably use a thousand words to try to describe how it is over here and never really quite explain it at all.

It won't be long now till Larry gets married and we'll finally get a girl in the family. I think a lot of Claudine and I think she will make Larry a good wife (I just hope he makes her a good husband). I guess Gary is still living the life of leisure and probably enjoying it very much. I do pray and hope that with everything that's happened our family becomes closer. We have had some good and bad times, but our love for you has always been there and it always will be! I will be a happy man if my children have the love and respect for me as I do for you. As a father I can only hope that I can do as good as you have.

If you sell the house will you take all of the fish with you? I'll bet with all of the bills there's not much left for yourself. You have never asked of us and I guess that's because a proud man never has any needs. The money I am making over here now I have no need for until I am out of the service. I can see no reason to let it just sit in a bank without being used. I could just as easily send it to you to help out in the rough spots. It won't be much. About $200 a month.

I have been looking around for different things over here and the only thing I found that you might be interested in is a shoulder holster for your '.45'. If you would like one, I will be glad to send it. I've got to go for now.

I love you very much.
Mike

Oh! About the radio. I had to pawn it before I left Okinawa due to financial difficulties. There was a key with my sea bag, but it must have come off. If you cut the lock off, inside you will find a picture of our platoon and a picture of our platoon party in an Okinawa bar.

VIETNAM—JUNE 1ST, 1966

Dear Dad,

Sorry it took so long for this reply, but we have been up on the mountains flushing out V.C.

The mountains are like a honeycomb and the flamethrowers we have been using sure come in handy! It's starting to rain just about every day for an hour or two and it sure is nice. During that time if we happen to be set in some place, we get a chance to take a bath!

The razor that was in my sea bag cost me $5. If you want it, it's yours. I won't have any use for it! I would send you the names of the guys in the picture but I could never remember where everyone was standing! I don't remember where this one guy was standing in the picture I sent you, but his name was Chapman and he looked like a rat. He sat down on a mine and they had to scrape him up into a bag! I can take pictures over here and I have written to Larry and Gary for a camera with no success. If you could take some money out of this check I have sent you and buy a Kodak Instamatic and some film it would be appreciated. There are some very beautiful scenes over here and also some interesting moments. I am not sending the shoulder holster right away because after getting a closer look at them they are pretty cheap and I want to look around for a better one.

You mentioned in your letter that you will have to work longer hours to make ends meet, just remember that your health is worth a lot more. I hope that everything is going fine at home and that the wedding is working out alright. I don't know when my next letter will be coming through but I will try to write soon.

Love Mike

VIETNAM—JUNE 15TH, 1966

Dear Dad,

I have just returned from Operation Apache Snow.[9] The operation took 5 days but very little V.C. were spotted. The first Calvary was over by the Cambodia border and they ran into a little trouble with the V.C's (200 were med-evac's). There is a good possibility that we might be going over there very soon.

There is also a touch of Malaria going around in the company, but I am doing O.K.[10]

By the sound of this letter it probably looks like things are pretty miserable over here, but actually things aren't too bad. By the time you receive this letter, Larry will probably be married and Father's Day will be over. I hope it was a Happy Father's Day and the wedding turned out alright.

Happy Father's Day!
Love Mike

---

9   Operation Apache was conducted by the 2nd Battalion, 5th Marines. It was classified as a search and destroy operation in the Quảng Trị Province.
10   Malaria sickened thousands of soldiers fighting in Vietnam. Of the four types of malaria, approximately 250,000 soldiers serving in Vietnam suffered cerebral malaria. Cerebral malaria causes depression, poor memory, personality change, and irritability/violence and, in some cases, partial seizure-like symptoms.

VIETNAM—JUNE 18TH, 1966

Dear Dad,

Today is payday and I'm glad to see half the month is gone! I thought I would be able to send $200 a month home, but it looks like it will be running a little lower. Larry wrote and said that the two of you finally got the bike matter squared away for me. I would like to thank you very much for that. Well, the wedding is over and Larry is now a married man. How was the wedding? Did they have liquor at the reception? We're now on standby for another operation.

    We don't spend much time on the top of this hill. Every time we come in they send us right back out. This operation is going to be about ten days long and then July will be here. Time sure is going fast, but I imagine that it will start slowing down!

    I've got to go for now, but I'll write again soon. I love you and I'll see you in "7" months.

                                                                          Mike

VIETNAM—JUNE 23RD, 1966

Dear Dad,

Right now I'm sitting up at the Battalion Aid Station with bandages on my feet. I caught a little piece of shrapnel in my foot and it got infected. Nothing to worry about though. One good thing about it, I'll be out of the field for a few days. We got hit pretty hard the other night, but we also hit back just as hard. We had two people killed and 17 wounded. The V.C lost about 30 men. We don't know exactly because they drag off their dead.

I imagine Larry is married and on his honeymoon by now. How was the wedding? Aunt Lura wrote and said she would be with you at the wedding, but didn't say if she would be staying there for any length of time. Who did Gary bring to the wedding and was she good looking?

I am sending you checks because it is easier than getting money orders. I had Larry withdraw the money from the account I'd already started. Did you receive it yet? I'm going to leave all of the bookkeeping up to you if that's alright.

I wish I had that camera I asked you about. I could've taken some really good pictures the other day. I'm going to close for now Dad, I'll see you in about seven months!

Love Mike

VIETNAM—JUNE 27TH 1966

Dear Dad,

Everything calmed down a little so they moved us back to hill "69". Hill "69" is where they have tents we can sleep under and get a hot meal. It's really not a bad place. There is a movie we can see at night and they just opened up a P.X. It's not too big, but it serves the purpose.[11]

The reason the money comes in different amounts is because sometimes I take a little out! I get paid twice a month, the grand total of $184.00.

When I don't need any money it's due to my good fortune at poker and my check will be $92.00. On the other hand if I lose or need to buy something then the check will be reduced. As for the next check when you receive it, it will only be for $60 because of the P.X. opening. As I wrote before, I would like to keep the bookkeeping up to you.

My base pay is $117.60 + $9.00 overseas pay + $65.00 combat pay = $191.60 minus Social Security, which is about $7.60.

As I said before, I am glad to have the Honda out of my name and to also have a lot of other things in the past. I did some foolish things that I'm ashamed of, but as you said they're in the past now.

I'm very anxious to see what the camera looks like and to start taking pictures. As I send you rolls, I'll tell you about them. There's only 1 thing. Some of the pictures will be of dead bodies. I don't know if they will develop them.

I'm glad to see that everything is working out fine at home.

---

11 PX is a retail store on US military installations for soldiers to buy things that are issued by the government during their station on base.

Tell Gary I will really enjoy receiving some cookies and I hope everything is going ok for him. Larry said Gary[12] bought a new car. How is it?

It looks like everyone that came into the Corp with me got easy jobs except me. Steve is an M.P. around the Helicopter AirStrip and Tom is riding around in a Tank at Da Nang.

Oh! One thing I wanted to ask you. What is going to happen to the cabin? Are you and the Rormarts still on good terms?

It won't be long till I'm home - just six more months!

With all my love,
Mike

---

12 Michael Gordon has two older brothers: Gary, the eldest, and Larry, the middle child.

Carrying bodies of soldiers killed in battle.

Helicopter setting down for pickup of soldiers.

VIETNAM—JULY 5TH, 1966

Dear Dad!

I'm sorry to have worried you as much as I have, but there was very little injury to my foot. In fact, 2 days after it happened I was back in the field. The pieces tore my jungle boot up quite a bit, but didn't enter my foot too far. There were several pieces on the top of my foot and one in the rear!

Battalion Aid is set up on top of hill "69" and is permanent. It consists only of Navy Corpsman—no Doctors.[13]

All of the Doctor's are about 5 miles to the rear where there is a regular hospital. The only time you are taken to the hospital is when you are seriously injured.

Today we are moving out of the mountains to guard some ammo dumps in the rear. I don't know how long we will be there, but it looks like we won't be seeing any action for a while. I received the camera today and was very surprised by the expensive looks of it. The camera must have cost quite a bit with its automatic light exposure and all, but I can't figure out what the + and dial is for.

Yes, Sue does still have the television, but I am going to let her keep it due to the trouble she has been through. As far as the pictures and the book, I didn't know she had them. I'm almost positive that I left them in the spare bedroom!

If for some reason she does have them, I would appreciate it if you could get them back!

Well, I hope that everything is going fine at home and that I

---

13   Navy corpsmen provide direct support to Navy and Marine Corps commands, squadrons, battalions, and units. They are deployed in support of combat operations, disaster relief, and humanitarian assistance missions.

haven't worried everyone too much. If and when anything does happen I will be sure and tell you all of the details.

I love you very much,
Mike

VIETNAM—JULY 18TH, 1966

Dear Dad,

I received your birthday card and it was nice to know that you are backing me and praying for me all the way. Everything is still going ok and we are still guarding the ammo dumps. I have taken 18 pictures so far which you will receive shortly. Some of the pictures were taken while we were at the beach. Don't get the wrong idea, because the pictures will probably look like everything is just one big ball over here.

I haven't sent any money home because they didn't have any checks, so I left all of it on the books. At the end of the month you should be getting a check for $184.00. I won $180.00 playing cards the other night, so I'm going to live off of that for a while, and send all of my paychecks home!

I have been put up for promotion, but nothing is definite as of yet. If I make it I will be one of the few people to make E-4 in under one year in the Corp!

Did you find the pictures and the book you asked about? Have you seen Larry and Claudine and how are they doing?

Dad I've got to go for now, but I'll write again as soon as I can!

I love and miss you,
Mike

Michael at the ocean off the coast of Vietnam.

VIETNAM—JULY 19TH, 1966

Dear Dad,

It looks like we haven't been taken out of the action all together. We have just been put on condition yellow (hundred-percent alert) because we got word that V.C. are headed our way! It could be a false alarm. On the other hand it could be for real.

You said on the back of your Birthday card that you'd hoped everything arrived in one piece. If you mean the camera, yes, everything is in good shape!

As I mentioned before, I have already taken 18 pictures. I seem to have ran out of things to take pictures of because all there is is ammo and sand! We are going to be moving at the end of the month, so I will be taking more pictures. In my last letter that I wrote, I said you would be getting a check for $184.00. Well, I am going to leave it in the books for R & R.

I hope when I get to go on R&R it will be in Bangkok on the shores of Thailand. Today promotions come out so it won't be too long till I know one way or the other!

Dad, I hope that everything is going fine at home and that you're not working too much to get things squared away.

I love you and miss you,
Mike

VIETNAM—AUGUST 6TH, 1966

Dear Dad,

I still haven't received those brownies you sent but I am expecting them any day now. Here is a new role of film mainly of a patrol on Amtracks and on the landing zone for a new operation going on now. I won't be able to get any pictures while on the operation due to the fact that the camera is busted. It happened when a sniper opened up on us and I dove to the deck. I had the camera attached to my cartridge bolt so I could get to it easier and when I got up the case was broken along with the lens and electric eye!

I am going to have a friend buy me another one while in Japan on R&R. I think this time I am going to get the '704'. How did the other pictures come out? If it wouldn't be too much trouble I would like to know how much I have in the account, including what will eventually be there.

Based on the pictures you sent of the wedding, Gary has a good looking girl. I only hope I can find one as cute when I get home. Oh! The name of the operation we are on is "Colorado". Maybe you might hear something on the news about us. There is already quite a bit of action going on.[14]

Well I got to take out a patrol Dad!

I love you very much.
Mike

---

14   Operation Colorado or Operation Colorado/Lien Ket 52 was a joint operation between the US Marine Corps and Army of the Republic of Vietnam (ARVN) that took place in the Hiệp Đức District, the south central coast of South Vietnam, from August 6 to 22, 1966.

Michael took many photographs with this type of camera until it was shattered in battle.

VIETNAM—AUGUST 20TH, 1966

Dear Dad,

How is everything at home? OK I hope. I realize you are probably pretty busy. I thought you mentioned in one of your letters that brownies were on the way. If so, I haven't received them yet. We went out on Operation Colorado as a supporting element but were never called upon. I have been out of action for so long, I'm starting to get jumpy!

It may be a way to stay healthy, but after having the excitement of it all and then having none, it gets on my nerves! How did the pictures come out? I haven't been able to go on R & R yet and I doubt if I ever will. A friend of mine went on R & R, so I gave him $150 to buy me a new camera and some walkie talkies. I thought they could always be used while hunting back home. I have stopped gambling for a while. I figure I better quit while I am ahead!

I've got to go on a patrol. Will write again soon.

Love Mike

VIETNAM—AUGUST 28TH, 1966

Dear Dad,

I was so glad to receive your letter. I was starting to get concerned thinking something had happened. I realize it is not easy to sit down and scribe a letter, but I got worried as you do, thinking something might have happened.

Some of the pictures are of landscapes taken atop hill "69" and while on patrol. I believe these were of our campsites, but not being able to see them, I can't quite remember. The Amtracks are used mainly for river patrols and mount a 106 recoilless rifle on top. The Amtracks don't move very fast through water or on land, but they have no problem with deep water. They can be used to carry troops into battle, but the sides are not very thick. A .50 cal. machine gun can rip it apart. Their main design was for breach landing because the "Mike" boats could get across shallow reefs.[15]

That was a .50 cal. machine gun on top of the truck. They are used to protect our convoys! The missiles on that trailer were "Hawk Missiles" or sometimes known as "side-winders". When fired, they automatically seek out heat from the exhaust of a jet and destroy it. They are all around the border of Vietnam and assure us that the sky is ours!

I am not sending the remains of the camera home because I know longer have them. The side along with everything else was warped out of shape so that light could get to the film. I figured it would be just as cheap to buy a new one. Although the guy that

---

15   LVTP-5 Amtrac is an amphibious armored fighting vehicle used by the Marine Corps.

went on R & R to get me a new one said they haven't got them in Japan yet so he got me a 104 instead.

He did get the walkitalkies for me, but I haven't seen them as of yet. He left them on hill "69", but I hope to have them in use in a few days.

It takes about five days by Air Mail and about six or seven by regular mail. All the mail is flown into Vietnam. The only good thing about putting an Air Mail on a letter is that from Sacramento to San Francisco it is flown, not trucked. I haven't received the package as of yet but it shouldn't be long now. A lot of the guys get packages from time to time, but usually the things they get are so rare over here that they're gone before they know it!

For every piece of mail or roll of film I send home I have to put 8 cents worth of stamps, for what reason I haven't figured out yet. As far as dropping the 'L/Cpl' on my address, I am almost positive it will come in as Sergeant.

R & R is rest and relaxation. I have put in for Tokyo in September and it looks like I might get it! Tell Gary if he wants to shoot something so bad, I'll change places with him any day. Truly I hope both of you are successful in getting a buck and some. I hope to get one myself!

I am glad to hear that everything is going fine at home and that you can relax from your work a little.

I was very surprised but glad to see that you were growing a beard! I guess you really do have a new outlook on life. It looks like my father is turning into the town playboy, and it sounds great to me! Just remember if they're all too old, they can't be too young. You're not the only one who would complement you on your looks. Everyone says I look like you, so you know that you're pretty sharp!

Tomorrow we will be going to the villages and explaining about an election coming up in September. If the election goes the wrong way we might be out of Vietnam before too long. I would like to get out, but I don't want the Communist to come in.[16]

Well I've got to go.

I miss you very much,
Love Mike

Official US Marine Corps photo of an Amtrac LVTP-5 transport. Photo courtesy of the Kenneth W. Koldys Collection (COLL/5791) at the Marine Corps History Division.

---

16   The 1966 United States mid-term elections were held on November 8, 1966, and elected the members of the 90th United States Congress. The election was held in the middle of Democratic President Lyndon B. Johnson's second (and only full) term.

VIETNAM—AUGUST 31ST, 1966

Dear Dad,

Well the box you sent arrived yesterday and everything was in great shape except for the brownies, mold had formed between the layers. I ate and ate until I thought I'd bust. Everything tastes so good - thank you very much. I bought myself a birthday present, it is a Zenith Radio with 9 bands, model 3000-1.

It cost me $75, but I am sure it costs twice that in the States. I'm going to send this one home after I get a little use out of it. I can pick up the states on it at night. It sure sounds great to hear an American station.

Our battalion received the Presidential Citation yesterday so I will be wearing another ribbon when I get home. I sure would like to get a bronze or silver star, but I am never in the right spot.[17]

The next roll of film that you see will already be processed and paid for. I'll send the film to Kodak in Hawaii with the process pre-paid and they will mail it to you.

I would like you to send me a hundred dollar money order so when I go on R & R on the 18th of September I won't get caught short of money. I don't really plan on spending it, but I don't want to get caught short. In the months following you will be receiving all of my paychecks.

Well I meant for this to be a short letter and it is. I'll write again soon. All of my thoughts are of home and being able to see you again.

Love Mike

---

17   The Republic of Vietnam Presidential Unit Citation, also called the State of Vietnam Friendship Ribbon, was awarded to United States military units by the President of the Council of Ministers, State of Vietnam, for supporting the South Vietnamese army from the mid-1950s to the fall of South Vietnam in 1975.

VIETNAM/TOKYO—SEPTEMBER 15TH, 1966

Dear Dad,

I just returned from Tokyo and had the time of my life! I bought quite a few things while there. You will be receiving them in the mail. There is a desk set for both you and Gary, the rest of the things are for me but you may use them if you like. I took quite a few pictures. When I receive them I'll send them on to You!

I met a Japanese girl in Tokyo, about 5 ft - 92 lbs and very good looking. She treated me like a King. In fact, I think she fell for me. I went everywhere with her and most of the time she paid - old Japanese Custom! She brought back so many old memories along with giving me new ones. I only hope someday I can go back to see her and tell her how grateful I was.

Now I am back on top of hill "69" just waiting for the troops to come in out of the field. I wish I didn't have so much time on my hands to think about coming back home.

That's the one bad point of being over here. Sometimes you have too much time and it starts working on your mind.

Right now everything is still dreams, but soon it will turn into reality.

In about a week we will be going on a new operation. I don't know much about it yet but it should be a big one. The monsoon season is supposed to be here by now, but it's not raining any more than it does in California. If it stays this way I will be very happy.

I was just wondering what I'll do for transportation when I get home. Do you have any suggestions? I have been writing to girls in the states and I would like to be able to see them once in a while.

How is your beard coming along? If they didn't make us shave over here I'll bet I could grow a 'mustache'!

Well Dad as I said before it won't be too long before I'll be phoning you to pick me up at the airport.

See you soon.
Love Mike

VIETNAM—SEPTEMBER 25TH, 1966

Dear Dad,

Well you finally caught me with 2 letters to answer! The "Gordon" written on my helmet is for identification purposes only. This new camera I got has no shutter speed adjustment or light focus. The only thing I can do is just hope the conditions are right. The only reason I took those moving pictures at right angles is because I wanted to get close to the subject!

As far as Japan goes it is all just memories now, but being over here for so long without being able to let it go. It just made it that much better.

Not too many of the guys over here are able to get their sexual feelings satisfied because of a disease we call the 'Black Sif'!

There is no cure for it and sooner or later you will die. If you get it, a letter is sent home stating that you are missing in action. All of your communication with the states is cut-off. You just rot away. I was talking with the Chaplain last month and he said, "three people were taken to the hospital with this disease just three days before."[18]

As I said before, we were due to go on another operation. By the time you receive this letter I will be out hunting V.C. The rains are coming every night now so this one should be a dilly!

It is only transportation that I want so the English Ford will be fine. I didn't think Gary would go for me using his car. If I can, I

---

18   Black syphilis proliferated throughout the Asian world and among American military personnel during the Vietnam conflict, although strangely very few known bonafide cases have been medically documented. Today, the disease is rumored to exist primarily in Thailand. In the American military, it was rumored that should a person contract the dreaded disease abroad that they would be forbidden from reentering the US.

would just as soon drive the Jeep.

When I went on R & R, I had to borrow money from a friend of mine, so I gave him the money order in payment and he sent it home.

I will keep you informed on when I will be arriving in Sacramento so you can be there to see the plane come in and I won't have to wait impatiently to see you.

See you in about 132 days

All my love,
Mike

OCTOBER 1966

The Vietcong's 9th Division, having recovered from battles from the previous July, had been preparing for a major offensive. Losses in men and equipment have been replaced by supplies and reinforcements sent down the Ho Chi Minh trail from North Vietnam.

VIETNAM—OCTOBER 1ST, 1966

Dear Dad,

You know that operation I told you that we were going on, it has been canceled. We are now Phu Bai, about twenty miles north. The 7th Marines got their ass kicked up here so we have been brought in to take their place. A lot of people that came over with 2/5 were transferred to the 7th Marines.

All of them are dead now from what I hear. I just hope the same thing doesn't happen to us. If I was to say I wasn't afraid, I would be lying because the shit really is hitting the fan up here!

I probably won't be able to write for a while so don't expect too many letters. We will be there for about sixty days if everything goes alright.

The 17th parallel which is shown as a dotted line on the map below is the area that we will be in. It's too close for me to come home for anything to happen now, so pray that my luck holds out!

Just remember I love you very much and I always have.

See you soon.
Mike

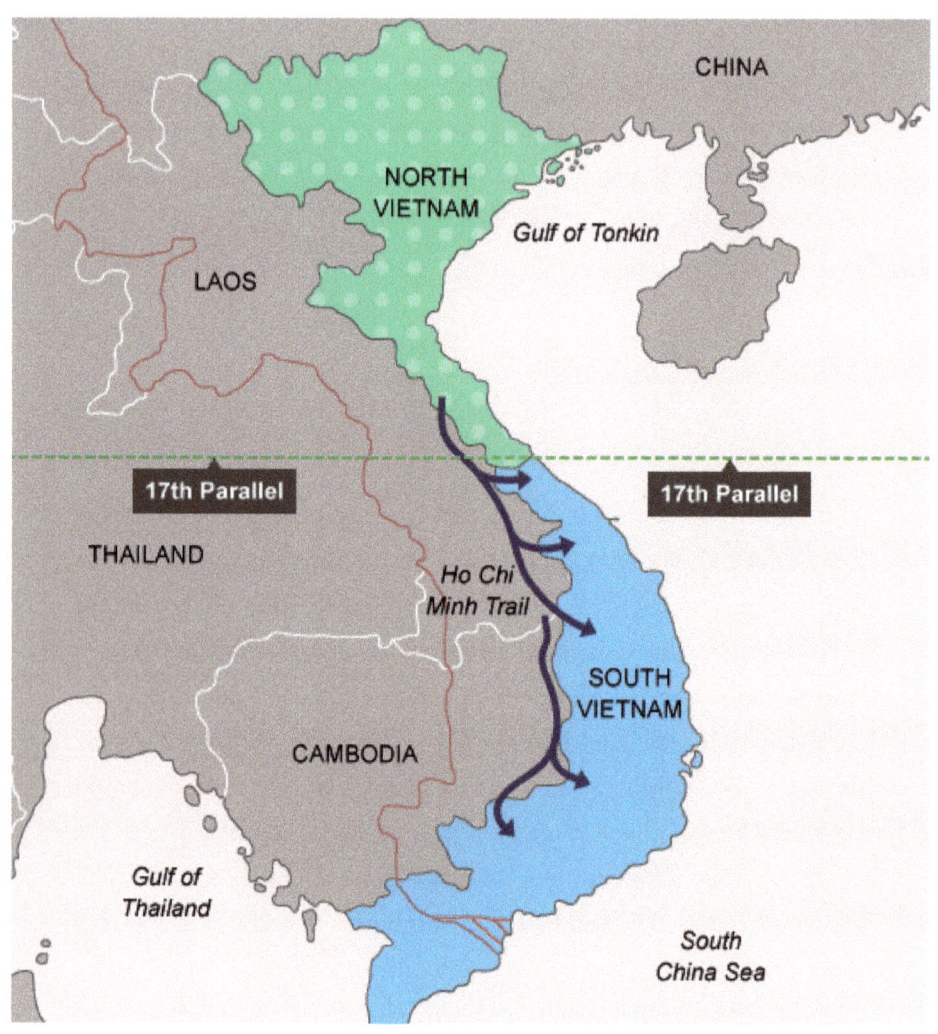

Map, courtesy of ResearchGate.

VIETNAM—OCTOBER 11TH, 1966

Dear Dad,

We're on operation Prairie and everything has gone fine so far. We have gone so far as three-hundred meters on the North side of the 17th parallel!

One of the company's with us has taken quite a few casualties, but we have been very lucky so far. They say that this operation could last until the end of the war, but I doubt it very much. It has been raining quite a lot lately, but I think we've seen the worst.[19]

I don't think we will be getting paid till the 1st of November, but from now on I'm going to try to send a bit of my money home. By the time I reach the states, I hope to have about $1,500. That is if I don't get promoted. Speaking of promotions, they say there won't be pay this month because of the operation. There has also been talk of moving to Da Nang and letting the Vietnamese Army take over Chu Lai.[20]

Thanksgiving is not too far away and I'll bet the rest of the stores have Christmas displays already! I wish I could spend the holidays home with my family, but maybe next year.

I haven't been able to write to everyone so tell Larry and Gary that I'll try and write soon.

---

19   Operation Prairie was a US military operation in Quảng Trị Province, South Vietnam, that sought to eliminate People's Army of Vietnam (PAVN) forces south of the Demilitarized Zone (DMZ). Over the course of late 1965 and early 1966, the Vietcong and the PAVN intensified their military threat along the DMZ. The tactical goal of these incursions was to draw United States military forces away from cities and towns.
20   Chu Lai Air Base was a military airport in Chu Lai, South Vietnam, operated by the United States Marine Corps between 1965 and 1970. Abandoned after the end of the Vietnam War, it was reopened as Chu Lai Airport in 2005.

Did you receive the record player, field glasses and disk sets I sent? Also did you receive the Zenith Radio and what shape was it in? I wouldn't have bought those things, but I got such a good buy on them that I couldn't pass them up.

I know this letter is hard to read but my thumb still hasn't healed from where I had the warts burnt off.

Give my love to everyone and I hope that everything is fine.

See you soon.

Love Mike

VIETNAM—OCTOBER 22ND, 1966

Dear Dad,

Well I finally made E-4 and it sure feels great. The warrants were dated the 1st of the month so I almost have a month in grade!

We have been operating up by the 17th parallel for twenty-two days now. There is quite a bit of action going on and we have had our share. We never know where the V.C. are or when they're going to hit. This is all jungle area and a V.C. could hide three feet away and you would never know he was there. They're real shots so when they hit, somebody usually dies.

We have only four dead and nine wounded out of our platoon so far, but other platoons have as many as twenty dead and the same number of wounded. When 'G' company came back the other day, out of 2 squads there were only five people left.

We are killing about 10 V.C. to every Marine, but still a Marine is dead. We have been up here for twenty-two days so far and we might stay till the end of December!

I have some film to send home, but no stamps. How about sending six airmail stamps? I have not been able to get any action shots with my camera, because when the action starts I have to control my squad, not a camera. Then when it is all over, we get out of the area as fast as possible. It has been raining for the past three days.

I'm starting to wonder if this is the beginning of the end.

The holidays will be coming up soon. I hope they are happy ones for our family.

Take care,
Love Mike

VIETNAM—NOVEMBER 7TH, 1966

Dear Dad,

By now you know that I have been trying to get emergency leave to come home early. I received a letter five days ago from Sue Kershaw and enclosed was a paper clipping about Thelda.[21] Yesterday I received your letter confirming the article. There are quite a few reasons for my wanting to come home. If I do get leave, I don't have to come back. By coming home now they will move my rotation date forward and my tour will be over.

Right now I have been taken out of the field and I am waiting in Chu Lai to see if I will get my leave. It was hell up at the D.M.Z. The guys were getting dinged left and right. I didn't want to leave my squad, but there is no way of knowing if you will be living tomorrow!

I would really like to see Thelda. I know she has done a lot of damage to our family, but she has also taught us a lot of things that you cannot learn in school!

I don't hate her Dad. I'm just awfully glad we have you back! Maybe my heart is too big Dad, but it's been a long time since I've given any love.

If you have not received a package with some boots and utilities in it, you will. Also in this package is a V.C. grenade that I took off one of the V.C. that I killed. It is pretty harmless now but don't mess with it! I'll tell you the whole story when I get home.

---

21   Thelda Gordon was convicted of embezzling $8,162 from Contractor Lumber Sales.

I just may see you for Thanksgiving I hope. Tomorrow or the next day I should have the final word. If I do come, I 'll call you and let you know when my flight will arrive.

Hope to see you sooner than we thought!

Your ever loving son,
Mike

P.S. Buy the camera there!

Sacramento Socialite Given Prison Term for Grand Theft

Thelda Marie Gordon, a former secretary of the Grand National Horse Show, has been sent to state prison for grand theft.

Mrs. Gordon, 51, associated with Sacramento philanthropies and frequently pictured in the city's social news pages, pleaded guilty to embezzling about $8,000 over the past year from the Contractor Lumber Sales in Carmichael, where she worked as a bookkeeper.

When her employer hired an auditor to find out why the company was not making as much profit as it should, Mrs. Gordon left and committed herself to DeWitt State Hospital.

She was arrested and brought back from DeWitt after the audit revealed she had been altering checks and the books and failing to make bank deposits.

The probation report on Mrs. Gordon disclosed she had borrowed about $30,000 from friends over the past two years.

Mrs. Gordon, once secretary of the Grand National Horse Show in San Francisco, was thought by her friends as "charming, generous to a fault, exquisitely groomed and socially correct, the perfect, impeccable hostess." And "they still refuse to believe the charges are true," said the probation officer who questioned many of them about her.

"There seems no likelihood," he said, "she could ever repay the huge sums of her friends' money which she has lavishly spent and gambled away."

Walter Pfister, Mrs. Gordon's employer as Contractor Lumber Sales, said, "She's taken advantage of everyone who thought so much of her and tried to protect her."

She was leading "a double life," declared Sacramento County Superior Court Judge William M. Gallagher, who sentenced her.

Thelda Gordon's prison sentence for grand theft carries a maximum term of 10 years.

Thelda Gordon's sentencing on her embezzlement conviction ran in a November 1966, edition of the *Sacramento Union*.

VIETNAM—NOVEMBER 9TH, 1966

Dear Dad,

Yes! I did receive your letter and I can't figure out why it was sent back either. Hurray! Is right, but now I'm looking for E-5.[22]

I know I only have a few months in grade as an E-4, but if I do an outstanding job it's possible to get an E-5 before I leave Vietnam. Of course, If I should extend over here for six months, I would be sure to get promoted, but that doesn't sound too good.

As you can see I didn't get to come home! I guess it's OK though. I sure would have liked to get out of this place.

Tell you what Dad, when I get home I want to take a trip and see Aunt Lura and Uncle Arthur. How about just you and I making that trip? I realize it would mean taking a few days off of work, but I think we both deserve it!

How good of shape is the Dormarts V.W and if the price is right I just might want to buy it. Take a look at it and see what you think?

I wish you wouldn't worry so much about me. Just ninety more days and I will be there. Anyway, these V.C.s are more afraid of me than I am of them (I think)! As it stands right now, I'll be going back to the D.M.Z zone in about seven days. That's where I'll either make it or break it, and as sure as I am "I'll make it"!

I don't know what's happening to those two brothers of mine, but they're missing the beat somewhere. What's Gary's military status?

I could use some more film. I haven't had a chance to buy any

---

22   E-5 refers to the pay grade for the rank of sergeant in the Marine Corps and indicates a certain level of experience and responsibility within the military hierarchy.

lately! I'm sending one roll of film directly to you and one roll to Hawaii to be developed. Also I am sending you some pictures I developed while I was in Tokyo. I am missing one roll of film though.

The F in front of the ⅖ means "F" Company. Have you played the record player yet? If you have time I would like you to stop in at "National Radio Store", and price the external power unit adapter. There is also an adapter for the "Zenith Radio". I think I put that $1.05 in that Bank about three years ago. It was just to keep my account open. If you are ever down in that area, see if you can draw it out for me. If not, then don't worry about it.

You think you could use some pussy? How do you think I feel? At least you get to look at some. The stuff running around here stinks so bad, and looks so dirty that you don't even want to touch it with a ten foot pole! Oh! That reminds me, we had a guy get run up the other day for being a queer. One of the guys woke up one night, and this other guy was working out on his rod. Boy did the shit hit the fan. The whole place was in an uproar!

Well Dad I've got to go for now,
See you in "90" days.

All my love,
Mike

Michael (right) with members of his platoon.

VIETNAM—NOVEMBER 12TH, 1966

Dear Dad,

That woman back east that took her letters from her son to the papers, her name doesn't happen to be Mrs. Fountain? I'm glad the letter got published but let's just hope everything is ok. I know these supplies were from Berkeley but we have no way of proving it now.[23]

Dad. I don't think that I will extend over here for just another Strip or anything else!

I have written many letters to Larry and Gary asking each of them what's going on between them and you! They say everything else except what I ask them. I think they feel that if they say anything to me that I will turn around and tell you.

In the picture you sent me you look great Dad. I cannot wait to get home! That picture Dad, just seeing you again makes me want to come home so bad! I really miss you.

The guy I mentioned getting queer with the other one was while I was waiting for leave. I guess you're right about him probably enjoying it because I think if someone was to touch me in the middle of the night, I'd know it before he got that far!

I wish you would thank Mr. Yokum for me, and tell him as it stands right now, everything is supposed to be confidential as far as we're concerned. I mean there is no way I can give him any proof.

This boy named Fountain had to go up before the Battalion commander, but I haven't heard what happened. He sent a letter

---

23   Medical supplies and funding were said to have been sent to the Vietcong from Berkeley College, although the university in Berkeley, California, is University of California, Berkeley. Most crates were stamped: DONATED TO THE PEOPLE'S REPUBLIC BY YOUR FRIENDS AT BERKELEY COLLEGE.

about Berkely home to his mother and I guess she really went to the top with it.

Although I haven't been able to go anywhere. I'm still in the rear with my gear waiting to get back to my unit. I had a physical while I was just sitting around and the Doctor said that both of my eardrums have ruptured. They might have been this way ever since I joined the Corp. I know I had trouble hearing my Drill Instructor out of my left ear. The left one is supposed to have a big hole in it, but the right one just has a little hole. The Doctor said they were growing back together and is going to examine me again sometime this month.

Got to go for now Dad!

All my love,
Mike

VIETNAM—NOVEMBER 23RD, 1966

Dear Gary,

I guess everything is pretty well messed up around home, huh! Have you heard anything on why Thelda took the money? Have you seen very much of Dad or Thelda? What are you going to do for a job now that you have quit the hospital? How are Larry and Claudine working out? As you probably have heard I was trying to come home on emergency leave, but the red cross turned me down! It got me out of the field though so I'm pretty glad of that. I had a physical and the Doctor said that both of my eardrums are ruptured. I thought I might get to come home because of my ears, but they said my ears are starting to heal up so there is no reason to send me to the states!

Boy, you can't believe how bad I want to get out of here. Thirteen months is a long time to live away from the finer things in life! I know it's only a little over two months till I'll be home, but that seems like forever right now.

How's the female situation around town now? With all of the people they have been drafting it should be pretty good! I hope everything is going fine for you. I'll be seeing you soon.

Take Care,
Mike

P.S. Tell Dad not to print that article. One guy already got in trouble for having it printed! The Marine Corp says that's confidential material! I could lose my stripes—urgent.

VIETNAM—NOVEMBER 25TH, 1966

Dear Dad,

I know I wrote and said that I wish an article could be printed on the medical supplies from Berkley but I thought all of this was already out in the open. One of the guys wrote home to a newspaper about Berkley and now he may lose his stripes! I guess everything that goes on over here is supposed to be confidential, even the conditions we live in. I appreciate all of the trouble you have gone through but if it's printed I could be in big trouble. If Mr. Yokum has already printed, then we'll just have to wait and see what happens. It would be great to have it printed all over the papers and maybe stop the supplies, but I guess I figured wrong - huh? Well here's some more money for our account! I'll write again soon.

All my love,
Mike

Marine's Letter Raises Question Of Enemy Aid From University In US

Somewhere in Viet Nam an embittered Sacramento Marine believes a college in the United States is sending medical aid to the Viet Cong at the expense of America's fighting men.

Cpl. Michael J. Gordon explained his bitterness in a letter to his father, John W. Gordon of 4434 El Camino Ave., this way:

"I don't know what the people back there are doing but it's not helping our cause any. It's pretty discouraging to know that the people you're fighting for are helping the enemy."

Gordon said "a lot" of these medical supplies had been captured from the Viet Cong by a Marine unit. He said the markings on the packages bore the name of an American college.

Official Okay?

Further examination has revealed the supplies may have been prepared by a religious school in New Haven, Conn., and forwarded by a Yale University faculty group with the government's consent.

The Yale group, made up of faculty members who are representatives of the New Haven Young Friends, a Quaker order, had asked permission to send the supplies to North Viet Nam.

The government consented, hoping the supplies would help lead to contact with American prisoners of war in North Vietnamese prison camps. Government officials placed a limit on the amount of supplies that could be sent and stipulated those purchased must not be American supplies.

The plan has been criticized by some who feel the medical aid might return wounded Communists to action.

The senior Gordon, an ex-Marine who was aboard the Colorado during the Japanese attack on Pearl Harbor 25 years ago, said he believes his son is not aware of the government's plan, if such is the case.

"He might be under the impression they (the supplies) are coming from an American college," said Gordon, a construction foreman. He said his son's resentful note may have been deepened by a narrow escape he had from Viet Cong bullets.

Clash With Enemy

The 21-year-old Marine wrote his father that he was darting across an open field when two

Cpl. Michael J. Gordon

Viet Cong opened fire with automatic weapons.

"He (the enemy) was about eight feet away," the Marine said. "How he missed I'll never know, but bullets tore up everything around me."

Gordon returned the fire and later discovered the bodies of two fallen Viet Cong guerrillas. He said two men in his squad were wounded in the encounter.

Gordon, a 1963 El Camino High School graduate and former American River College student, has been in Viet Nam since April. His father said his son is due to return to the U.S. within 60 to 90 days.

Michael's letter and the story about it that he referred to in his letter above ran in the Nov. 20, 1966, edition of the *Sacramento Bee*.

VIETNAM—DECEMBER 1ST, 1966

Dear Mom & Dad,

The holidays are just around the corner. I imagine that everywhere you look there is something pertaining to Christmas or the New Year. I can just see all of the houses lit up at night with their colorful light bulbs and displays. It's funny, but I wonder how many people at Christmas time are really thankful.

They still haven't told me anything definite as to where I'll be going when I leave the hospital, but the C.O mentioned something about me going home. How much truth there is to that is beyond me, but my luck will hold out if I don't press it too much.

I have thoughts of buying a new car when I arrive home, but I think I'm going to hunt around for a good used car.

Since I've been over here I've received one letter from Gary, that was because he knew I was in the hospital in Japan and he wanted me to buy him some stereo equipment. As for Larry I guess he's been involved in other things.

When I get home, I don't want to get involved with family affairs, each of us has our own problems.

It has been raining so hard around here for the past month and a half. I'm beginning to wonder if it is ever going to quit. On that last operation as we moved into an area one night, it rained so hard that the following morning we couldn't get off the high piece of ground we were on.

Say hello to Steve and Johnny for me.

Love Mike

VIETNAM—DECEMBER 14TH, 1966

Dear Dad,

Here's a little more to add to our account. I have been transferred from 2/5 to 3/9, and had to leave $206 in debts owed to me behind.

I have a good friend of mine collecting the debts for me, but I am not actually looking forward to ever receiving the money. But if by some chance you receive some strange money orders or checks made out to you, you'll know what they're for.

All of the debts are gambling debts anyway, so if I never get anything out of them I still won't be out anything!

I was transferred to 3/9 because they are going back to Okinawa the first part of January and that will get me out of the war zone. I have a good chance of coming home in January instead of February like the original plan. I have no definite word as of yet.

I am looking forward to going up to Oregon with you, so I do hope that you can get off work. I will keep in touch so you know exactly when I will arrive.

Sorry to cut the letter short but I have some working parties to take out. See you soon.

"50 days at the most"

All my love,
Mike

1967

From January to May 1967, North Vietnamese divisions launched heavy bombardments of American bases south of the DMZ—Khe Sanh, the Rockpile, Cam Lo, Dong Ha, Con Thien, and Gio Linh. American and South Vietnamese forces launch Operation Junction City, a seventy-two-day effort to destroy Vietcong bases and military headquarters north of Saigon. Hundreds of North Vietnamese soldiers were killed in multiple battles in the central highlands of South Vietnam.

VIETNAM—JANUARY 1ST, 1967

Dear Dad,

I just received word that I will be home before the 10th of February, so here's hoping that it's true. The reason I haven't written for a while is because there is nothing to write about - and I mean nothing!

Right now I am standing guard on P.O.W.'s[24] and that is about the worst duty anyone can get. In 22 more days I will be home. In the future, start expecting a phone call. See you soon Dad.

All my love,
Mike

---

24 POW (prisoner of war) is a person who surrenders to (or is taken by) the enemy in time of war.

VIETNAM—JANUARY 1ST, 1967

Dear Dad,

First of all I would like to thank you for the Christmas gifts and card! This isn't quite the place to celebrate Christmas, and New Years, but at least it brings me that much closer to home. I have a good chance of arriving home in January, but I still have no definite word. We were supposed to go to Okinawa with the 3/9, but now they tell us we'll be staying in Vietnam until we rotate! There seems to be some questions about what to do with us once the 3/9 leaves for Okinawa.

What did you do for the holidays?

One of those packages I sent home has a polaroid camera in it just in case you ever want to use it. As you can tell by the date on this letter, last night was New Years Eve. I believe I celebrated it in style. In fact upon my return to the tent I seemed to have agitated three negroes. I wasn't too bad until one of them got me from behind with a club. To make a long story short, I wound up with six stitches in my head. I still think they got the worst end of it because the Marine Corp ring I wear definitely did some damage!

The corpsman had to shave the hair from around the cuts, so if it hasn't grown out by the time I get home you'll know why.

Other than that everything is going fine. I should be home within the next thirty-five days!

See you soon.

All my love,
Mike

VIETNAM—JANUARY 13TH, 1967

Dear Dad,

I've been transferred again and it's the same old thing. Some of the guys have already left for the states, so I hope to be there before the end of the month! I'll keep you in touch. Till then I send all my love.

See you soon.
Mike

VIETNAM—MARCH 27TH, 1967

Dear Dad,

Thank you very much for the Easter card. I hope you had a better Easter than I did.

Walter Hoyt didn't happen to tell you what my insurance is going to cost me. I'm going to be coming home on the 31st of this month so I should be able to find out all about it. Also I have to get my regular driver's license. Tell Walter I need the whole insurance policy to get a sticker for my car!

I would've sent you some money, but I got into a little trouble in Mexico and the bail was pretty high. I had to pay it otherwise I would have been A.W.O.L and anything is better than that. I hope to have some money for you when I come home, but nothing is definite.

Well, I'll tell you all about it when I get there.

Love Mike

UNITED STATES MARINE CORPS BRONZE STAR MEDAL AWARDED—APRIL 9TH, 1967

In the name of the President of the United States, the Commanding General, Fleet Marine Force, Pacific takes pleasure in presenting the BRONZE STAR MEDAL to:

CORPORAL MICHAEL J. GORDON

UNITED STATES MARINE CORPS

For service as set forth in the following

CITATION:

"For heroic achievement in connection with operations against the enemy in the Republic of Vietnam while serving as a Fire Team Leader with the Second Platoon, Company F, Second Battalion, Fifth Marines, on 26 October 1966. During Operation Prairie, west of Dong Ha in Quang Tri Province, Corporal GORDON's platoon was subjected to intense automatic weapons fire and grenades from a large North Vietnamese Army force concealed in a trench line. In the initial burst of fire, several Marines were wounded and fell in an area exposed to enemy fire. Assigned to secure a portion of a medical evacuation landing zone, Corporal GORDON quickly deployed his fire team while directing their fire on the enemy. Observing a wounded Marine lying in the exposed area, he completely disregarded his own safety to direct the man to a covered position. While he was still under fire and observed another man in danger, he threw a grenade at one of the enemy and unhesitatingly ran to the aid of the Marine. Exhibiting uncommon courage and initiative, he succeeded in moving the casualty to safety. His heroic and selfless actions were responsible for saving the lives of two wounded Marines, greatly aided by his platoon in accomplishing its mission and inspired all who observed him. Corporal GORDON's bold initiative, inspiring leadership and loyal devotion to duty at great personal risk were in keeping with the highest traditions of the Marine Corps and of the United States Naval Service."

Michael receiving his Bronze Star Medal for heroism during Operation Prairie.

CAMP PENDLETON—JUNE 19TH, 1967

Dear Dad,

Sorry I couldn't make it home to be with you on Father's Day, but I hope you had a wonderful time anyway! I phoned Saturday to talk to you but Gary had said you just left. My car is getting fixed but I don't know how much it will cost. That rubber boot finally gave out so I figured I better get it fixed before something serious happens.

    I phoned Gary and told him to phone Kathie, but I guess he forgot. Kathie was up all night waiting for me!

    As you can see by my return address I picked up my next strip. The extra money will come in handy.

    I know this is a little late but "Happy Father's Day" to the best Dad in the whole world.

See you soon,
Mike

Return Address:
Camp Pendleton, Edson Range

CAMP PENDLETON—JUNE 28TH, 1967

Dear Dad,

Just thought I would drop you a line and let you in on the latest news. I am going to be stationed at Camp Pendleton as a coach on the rifle range! Our orders came in yesterday but so far we haven't received our flight dates. When I get to Los Angeles, I'll call home person to person for myself, and the time I tell the operator to call back will be the time my flight arrives in Sacramento!

There is word going around that we will only get twenty days leave instead of thirty. The Marine Corp has an order issued about the twenty days, but it's effective as of February 1st. and our orders have already been cut.

Tell Larry and Gary that I doubt I can do anything for them as far as stereo equipment goes, because I will only be in Okinawa 24 to 48 hrs.

I hope that you have plenty of "Scotch" on hand when I get home, because it's been a long time since I had any hard liquor.

Say hello to everyone for me, and tell them I will be home in about eight days. See you soon.

All my love,
Mike

1968

Two of the biggest battles of the war, Khe Sanh and the Tet Offensive, took place in 1968. From January 21 to July 9, 1968, North Vietnamese and Vietcong pummeled the Marine base at Khe Sanh. And on January 30, 1968, the Tet Offensive took place. A surprise attack on command centers in South Vietnam, the Tet Offensive results in heavy losses of life and a subsequent declining support in the US for the war.

VIETNAM—JANUARY 13TH, 1968

Dear Dad & Mom[25],

I've finally reached Vietnam, but haven't been assigned to an outfit yet. I'm waiting in Da Nang right now for a flight to Quang Tri. but it looks like it might be a few days before I get one. As of yet it still looks like I might be in a line outfit, but I still have hopes of changing that.

I arrived at Norton A.F.B with plenty of time to spare. I didn't fly out of there until eight o'clock that night.

Note: Norton A. F. B—Norton Air Force Base.

From Norton, we flew over Sacramento and headed to Alaska. I wasn't able to see any part of Alaska because by the time we left Norton till we landed in Okinawa it was complete darkness (19 hours). I stayed in Okinawa for three days and then flew here to Da Nang.

---

25 Michael's father divorced his former wife, Thelda, who was Michael's stepmother, and remarried. His new wife is named Betty.

I've been told that I will be up north around Phu Bai with 2nd Battalion, 1st Marines, but I don't know what Company.[26] Say hello to Steve and John for me.

All my love,
Mike

---

26 In late 1965, The 3rd Marine Division established its headquarters at Phu Bai Base.

VIETNAM—JANUARY 18TH, 1968

Dear Dad & Mom,

I've finally been assigned to an outfit after all this time. I'm still not in a platoon, but that will all come in due time. I tried to get something other than a line outfit, but they're so short on Sergeants that they won't let me go. We're in the process of moving to a camp about 60 miles north of Quảng Trị. I don't know how long we will be there, but it shouldn't be too bad. Just about all I've been doing when I'm not in charge of some working party is play poker. So far I've won about $130.00, as soon as I can get a money order I will send it home for safe keeping. I don't know when I'll get paid, but you will get the allotment, and the bond. I would appreciate it if you would clear up my debt with DeVons Jewelers. If you decide to keep the V.W. , the debt to Devons will cancel out any payment on the V.W. Have you seen Kathie? I'll write again soon.

All my love,
Mike

P.S. My new address is:
Sgt. Gordon M. J. 2158672
E Co. 2nd Bn. 1st Marines
F.P.6 San Francisco. California 96602
Send me that pack in the closet and those utility covers (hats) in the other closet.

VIETNAM—JANUARY 19TH, 1968

Dear Mom & Dad,

Just some money to deposit for me and say hello.

Love Mike

VIETNAM—FEBRUARY 8TH, 1968

Dear Dad and Mom!

We've finally done it. We're completely surrounded by fifteen-thousand V.C. We don't know when they are going to hit us, but it only seems a matter of time. I'm constantly checking the lines to make sure everything is alright. There is a chance that we could be pulled out of here before they hit, but I don't think it's very likely! If it's not artillery or sniper fire, it's something else they hit us with day in and day out.

Of course, for every round they send to us, we send two or three back in return.

I came down with dysentery two days ago, but I am feeling better now. I think it was because I am so run down. I'm only averaging two to five hours of sleep every day.

But like I said before, there is no man or bullet that's going to stop me from coming home.

I love you both and I hope that all the happiness in the world is with you now!

With love,
Mike

VIETNAM—FEBRUARY 16TH, 1968

Dear Dad and Mom,

I received your Valentine's card and letter, but not the package. Don't worry though. I'm sure it's just being held up due to our messed up mail service. I'm sorry for the delay between letters but I've got my hands full trying to run this platoon. I'm hardly getting any sleep as it is between checking lines and receiving enemy artillery every day! In one day we receive anywhere from twenty to one-hundred and twenty enemy artillery rounds. Tomorrow we are going on patrol approximately 12,000 meters along the D.M.Z. There are some fortified enemy bunkers which we have to destroy (They have enemy in them). It won't be easy, but I guess it's for a good cause.

    Tell Kathie not to worry, it takes a hell of a lot to get a Gordon! Sorry to cut it short, but I've got to get some sleep.

                                                         Love Mike

VIETNAM—FEBRUARY 25TH, 1968

Dear Dad and Mom,

Yesterday our bunker took a direct hit and I was blown about six feet but I'm ok. It's going to take a hell of a lot more than that to put me down. One of my men had a leg blown off from the hip down. He eventually died. A couple others had wounds from shrapnel but they weren't serious. We received about six-hundred to a thousand rounds of enemy artillery. When we get incoming artillery we can only sit in our bunkers and hope one doesn't come in to join us! It's really getting bad. I had to slap three of my men around because I found them in corners shaking and crying.

When you get incoming how can you tell a man not to worry up here?

A man in the platoon next to us had his helmet crushed on his head, at least he died instantly!

Actually I'm in good spirits for what's going on around me. I could use some 'scotch' in plastic containers though!

Well I've got to go on patrol. Tell everyone that I'm alright and tell Johnny I'll be there with his present!

All my love,
Mike

Michael in his barracks.

VIETNAM—MARCH 2ND, 1968

Dear Dad and Mom,

Everything is going just fine so far, I just hope it stays this way. Our Battalion is organizing a snatch team to go into North Vietnam and capture some V.C. for intelligence. Tomorrow I am going to look into this snatch team and possibly volunteer to become a member. I know it's going to be dangerous but it's what I want. It beats sitting on this hill getting blown to pieces from enemy artillery rounds.

I just sent you a check for $500, let me know if you receive it.

The Lieutenant I had for a Platoon Commander was sent to the rear for a desk job, now I have a Staff Sergeant for a Platoon Commander. He's an OK guy and all, but he just doesn't know what he is doing half the time. I'm always setting everything up and he gets the credit! I can understand his position, not wanting everyone to know his junior is doing all the work he's supposed to be able to do - but if he can't make it he shouldn't have the position.

Enough of my complaining for now, I just have to tell it to someone.

How about packing up some goodies in a box and sending them over my way! These "C" rations just aren't getting with the program.

Steve and Johnny want to know where I am stationed. I'm as far North as any unit can get. From the front of our lines, 600 meters out, is North Vietnam. There are bunkers, trenches, tanks, rockets with 500 lb warheads, mortars and it won't surprise me when the enemy starts using planes. So you can see why I am not too happy defending this hill to the last man. I'll admit that we have good weapons and lots of support, but it's going to be a hell of a fight!

The mail is so messed up over here with all of the fighting going on. I haven't received your package.

Hope everything is fine at home!

Love Mike

VIETNAM—MARCH 19TH, 1968

Dear Dad & Mom,

Everything is pretty quiet now that we have moved from Con Thien to hill C-2. The hill we occupy now is about the size of Con Thien but we have eight-inch guns here that support Con Thien and Khe Sanh.[27] The V.C have been trying to probe our lines at night, but as of yet with no success! We called in artillery on some last night and this morning found four dead.[28] Tom Knoble is less than five miles from me. I hope to be able to see him tomorrow. He was up to my hill once, but I was out on patrol and was unable to see him.

It started raining today and is now coming down like cats and dogs. It looks like our rainy season is lasting a lot longer than it should.

Did you receive the check I sent for $500? Kathie has my record player but not the camera.

Susan Dillman wrote and said her father had seen you recently, but didn't discuss any other part of the acquaintance. The time has been going by pretty fast so far, hope it keeps up. Say hello to everyone for me.

Love Mike

---

27   In late January 1968 with increasing PAVN pressure on Khe Sanh Combat Base and Route 9, 1st Battalion 9th Marines were transferred to Khe Sanh, and 3rd Battalion 4th Marines were moved to the Lancaster area of operations. Second Battalion 4th Marines were assigned to take over the 3/4's area of operations northeast of Con Thien, and on January 27, HMM-361 landed the first units near C-2; by the end of the day the entire battalion was deployed.

28   On March 16, Mike Company, 3/3 Marines, and Charlie Company, 1/4 Marines, clashed with another battalion-sized PAVN force. The two Marine companies called in artillery and air upon the PAVN, the bulk of which disengaged, leaving a company behind to fight a rearguard action. PAVN artillery from north of the DMZ answered the American supporting arms with a 400-round barrage of its own on the Marines. Marine casualties were two killed and nine wounded and 83 PAVN killed.

APRIL 1ST, 1968

The U.S. Army 1st Cavalry and Marine 3rd Division begin Operation Pegasus. Its objective was to reach and relieve the garrison at Khe Sanh, which had been under siege since January. The Marines at Khe Sanh went on the offensive.

VIETNAM—APRIL 4TH, 1968

Dear Dad and Mom!

Everything is still going fine. We are on a sixty day operation now, but it could change at any time. We haven't run into very many enemy troops, but their mines are getting us one by one. Yesterday, I lost one out of my platoon, and another platoon lost six!

The mail situation isn't too good, so if my letters slack off a little bit don't worry.

I'm glad the V.W. has been working out O.K. for you. I think I'll buy another one when I get home.

Say hello to Steve and Johnny for me!

Love Mike

VIETNAM—APRIL 8TH, 1968

Dear Dad,

Here is my tax return from the government. I would like you to fill out a short form for me and also sign my name. I pay tax on $2,193.52, and my tax is $191. They took out $217.30, so I should get back $16.30.

Everything is going alright so far except our mail is messed up. I received Betty's letter saying you had written but I haven't received your letter yet. Tell Kathie not to worry, I guess she has been giving you a hard time.

Did you get the film and the one-hundred dollars? If Kathie needs money to buy goods to send to me would you give it to her out of my account? Give my love to Betty and the rest of the family and tell Betty I appreciate the letter from her.

Love Mike

VIETNAM—APRIL 13TH, 1968

Dear Dad & Mom,

I know this letter won't reach you by Easter, but I hope you had a happy one! Tomorrow is Easter Sunday and here I am sitting atop a mountain wondering where we're going next. The next roll of film will show you the size of the mountains we climb.

Speaking of film, I need some. I am on my last roll and unable to buy any. Along with the film I could use some goodies - salami, cookies, scotch in plastic containers and so forth! Oh, don't forget the mixer (Soda)! As you can see I am in pretty good spirits even though I am not a second Lieutenant. Maybe they'll give me E-6 instead. Promotions for E-6 come out in June!

Being a platoon commander and not getting paid for it is for the birds. I don't mind the job and have no trouble handling it but I wish I was getting paid what the other platoon commanders get paid. Right now I get $246 base pay and they get something around $430 base pay. Oh, well such is life.

Did Gary go into the service? And if so for how long and which branch?

Did Claudine file for divorce and if so, what is Larry doing now?

Did you get the house sold on El Camino or are you still fixing it up?

As things stand now I'll be home before February of next year unless I decide to extend. I'll probably be going on R&R in June to meet Kathie in Hawaii! If you can help Kathie in anyway please do so. It isn't easy for her to be at home all this time.

Say hello to Steve and Johnny for me.

Love Mike

APRIL 1968

Following the relief of Khe Sanh Combat Base in Operation Pegasus, the 3rd Marine Division resumed responsibility for Khe Sanh Combat Base and Operation Scotland II began. Marines sought out the People's Army of Vietnam (PAVN) forces on the Khe Sanh plateau, which comprises the western third of Quảng Trị Province.

VIETNAM—APRIL 18TH, 1968

Dear Dad and Mom!

My luck has finally run out. I'm now in a hospital at Phu Bai. Tomorrow I will be shipped to Cam Ranh Bay for further treatment.

Yesterday we were helo-lifted to Khe Sanh. I was only there for about three hours when we started receiving enemy mortars. The first round got myself and two of my radio men. A piece of metal went clean through my thigh. No bones broken. I'm in pretty good shape so don't worry!

I'll probably be back in the field in about one month. I told the Red Cross not to notify you because they don't give any details. You would be worrying if you received their letter.

All my love,
Mike

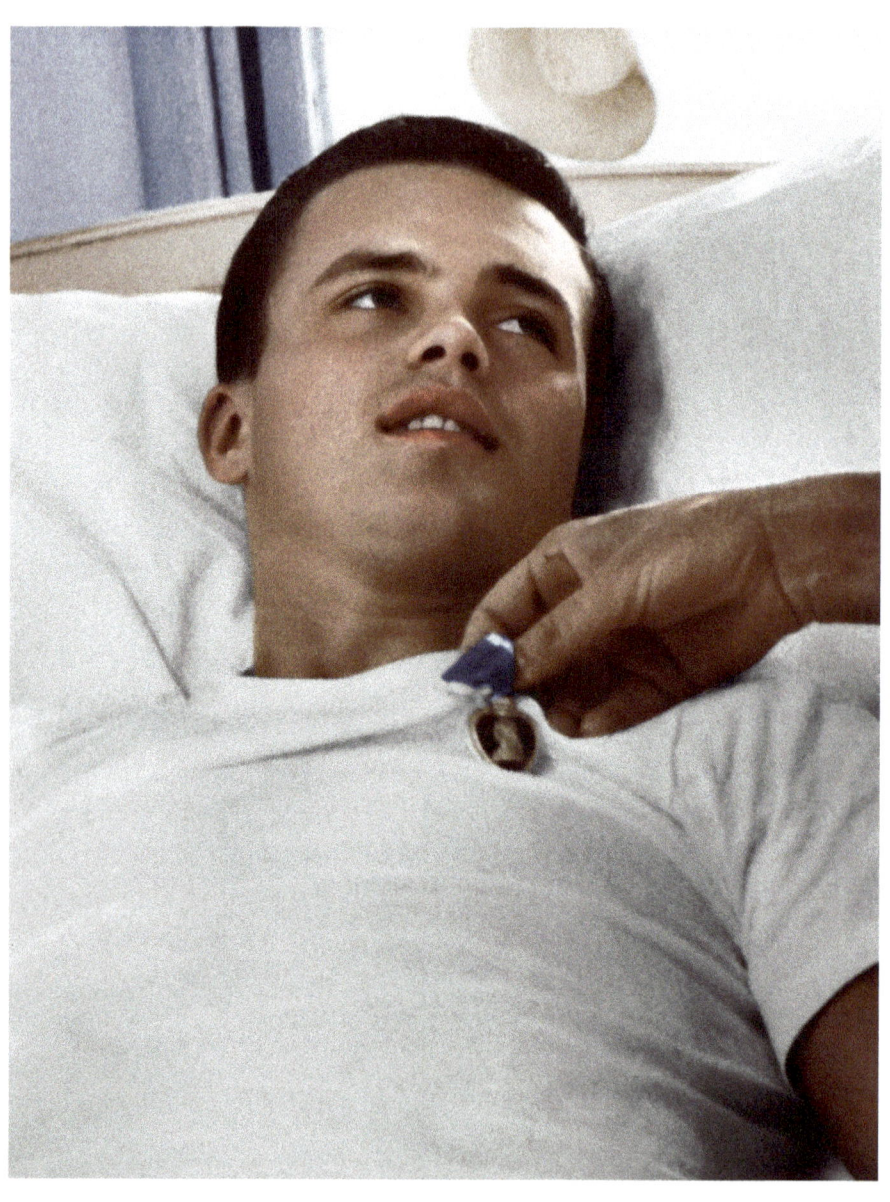

In his hospital bed, Michael receives one of his two Purple Heart medals for heroism in battles.

VIETNAM/OKINAWA—JUNE 4TH, 1968

Dear Mom & Dad,

Just a short note to tell you I am now in Okinawa on my way back down south. I should be here for three to seven days.

Yesterday, one of the guys from the platoon, the Lieutenant that took over for me, only lasted five days. They were out on patrol by Khe Sanh and an N.V.A machine gun sighted in on him. I guess I was pretty lucky to get hit when I did.[29]

I hope everything is going all right at home. Tell Steve and Johnny hello for me.

Write again soon,
Love Mike

---

29 The Battle of Khe Sanh began on January 21, 1968, when forces from the People's Army of North Vietnam (PAVN) carried out a massive artillery bombardment on the Marine Corps combat base at Khe Sanh in northwestern Quảng Trị Province, South Vietnam. The main US forces defending Khe Sanh were two Marine regiments assisted by troops from the US Army and Air Force, as well as troops of the Army of the Republic of Vietnam (ARVN). These were pitted against two to three divisional-size elements of the PAVN. For the next 77 days, US Marines and their South Vietnamese allies fought off an intense siege of the garrison, one of the longest and bloodiest battles of the Vietnam War.

VIETNAM/OKINAWA—JUNE 14TH, 1968

Dear Dad & Mom,

Just a short note to say "Happy Father's Day", I wish you all the happiness in the world.

I am still in Okinawa and will leave the 16th for Vietnam. Here's some more money to add to my little collection.

All my love,
Mike

VIETNAM—JUNE 19TH, 1968

Dear Dad & Mom,

I'm now back in Vietnam and at the D.M.Z waiting for my unit to return to Khe Sanh. I don't know whether I'll get back with my old platoon or even what my job will be. There are quite a few staff and officers now so I'll probably have to drop in ranks. I found out that I was written up for staff sergeant, but no word has come back from C.M.C yet.

Say hello to everyone for me!
Mike

VIETNAM—JUNE 25TH, 1968

Dear Dad & Mom,

I'm still at Khe Sanh, but should be leaving in the next month. We are now in the process of destroying Khe Sanh. When we leave here there will be no signs of life ever being on this hill.

I hate to leave though because of all the lives it took to establish this base. Did you receive all of my personal gear, if so please send me my camera and keep the rest. When I was medevac, they said they sent all of my personal gear to my home address.

I should be going on R & R in August to meet Kathie. I may need some of my money sent home. If so, I will let you know and Kathie can bring it with her. The reason for this is my pay record was also sent some place and it may not get back in time. If you receive my pay record and health record please send those also.

Say hello to the family for me.
Love Mike

VIETNAM—JULY 1ST, 1968

Dear Dad,

I believe they sent all of my mail to your address. If so, would you forward it to me in one bundle?

I will be leaving the Sang on the fourth of July. I hope there won't be any fireworks. We are going to walk the coast by Dong Ha.

I will be going to R & R in July to Hawaii, still don't know if I will need any money. I will probably phone you when I reach Hawaii but don't know the exact date.

Take care!
Love Mike

VIETNAM—JULY 15TH, 1968

Dear Dad,

The area I'm in is so secure. I haven't a worry in the world. We go swimming every day and have 1 hot meal per day.

Have you received my pay and health record? Have you received any letters from Thelda addressed to me?

Can you tell me how much money is in my account?

I will have Kathie get some of my clothes to bring to Hawaii with her. Also give her $500 dollars.

Love Mike

VIETNAM—JULY 24TH, 1968

Dear Dad & Mom,

Thank you very much for the birthday card, I really enjoyed it. Holidays and birthdays don't mean much over here unless your loved ones acknowledge you with a special note or card.

Those letters I wrote addressed to Dad only were because the letters contained only business matters. I thought it was pretty well understood how I felt about Betty before I left. My feelings have not changed.

I will be leaving here on the 24th of August to meet Kathie on R & R. I can hardly wait for the days to pass by.

The area that I am in now is around Dang Ha and I don't think there is a V.C for miles. We patrol every day, but we also get a swim call and a hot meal each day! Sometime around the middle of next month we will be moving to Da Nang for a while. It looks like the rest of my tour is going to be pretty pleasurable.

Did you know that Mrs. Yokum passed away? I wrote them a letter, but didn't know if you knew. Say hello to Steve and Johnny for me!

Love Mike

P.S. Has any of my gear arrived home?

VIETNAM—AUGUST 6TH, 1968

Dear Dad & Mom,

Not much is going on. Just waiting for my R & R date to roll around. We will be moving to Da
 Nang on the 20th of this month. Should be some good duty! Check and see if you can find that
 Polaroid camera of mine and send it. Kathie will be stopping by to pick up some money from you.

Love Mike

P.S. Please send some film with it.

VIETNAM—SEPTEMBER 2ND, 1968

Dear Dad & Mom,

I know you'll receive this letter after the happy occasion is over, but I still want to wish you a "Happy Anniversary". I know with Aunt Lura and Uncle Arthur there, the four of you must have had a good time. I wish you all the love and happiness in the world.

Hawaii was just terrific. Kathie and I had the time of our life there. I gave Kathie a bottle of scotch to give to you that I bought in Guam.

I arrived back to my unit on the 1st and I am already back in the field. This area we're in now is outside of Da Nang and has quite a few booby traps as well as N.V.A. The unit we relieved lost 800 men due to booby traps alone.

Did Larry and Gary get a chance to see Lura and Arthur? Tell Larry I enjoyed seeing the picture of his daughter. I only wish things could have worked out for them.

All my love,
Mike

VIETNAM—OCTOBER 10TH, 1968

Dear Dad & Mom,

Yesterday was like any other day except someone tried to kill me. Someone in my platoon threw a grenade at me. I only received a few fragmentations, nothing serious. I think I know who it was but I have no proof. I'll just have to wait and see what happens. Don't worry though. I'm sure I can handle anything that should come up.

We will be moving to Da Nang between the 15th and the 20th of this month. I'm sort of looking forward to some slack days for a while.

Say hello to the family for me.

Love Mike

P.S. Give that camera to Kathie. She'll give it to me on R&R.

VIETNAM—OCTOBER 20TH, 1968

Dear Mom & Dad,

Everything is still going just fine over here, with a little bit of action now and then. The monsoons have arrived and it doesn't seem like it will ever stop raining. Most of my time is spent in the field, but every once in a while I get to the rear to dry off. I'm only about 10 miles South of Da Nang, but have yet to get to the city itself. Tomorrow my platoon will be going to work with the South Vietnamese Armed Forces (Arvans). The biggest problem we have is with enemy mines and booby traps. Chesty Puller's son just got blown up by a booby-trapped 155 mm shell. He was one of our officers.[30]

Well in just three months I'll be on a plane headed home for good this time! Say hello to the rest of the family for me.

Love Mike

---

30 Lewis Burwell "Chesty" Puller, a Marine Corps officer, is the most decorated Marine in American history. He was awarded five Navy Crosses and one Distinguished Service Cross. Puller's son, Lewis, while serving with 2nd Battalion, 1st Marines, was severely wounded by a mine explosion, losing both legs and parts of his hands.

VIETNAM—NOVEMBER 10TH, 1968

Dear Dad & Mom,

Today is the Marine Corps Birthday, but it's no different than any other day. In fact, none of the holidays mean much over here. The monsoons have arrived and right now I am covered head to toe in mud. I thought I was through playing in the mud a long time ago. I guess someday I'll never have to be dirty and wet again. We are due to go on an operation tomorrow in a pretty hot area, but I am not expecting anything serious to happen.

Our biggest problem is going to be with mines and booby traps. It's the same area Chesty Puller's son had his legs blown off.

I'm not worried though, they haven't got me yet and they better be pretty good to get me at this stage of the game.

I haven't received my flight date yet, but I should be home by the 1st of February. I hope to get my orders for my next duty station by the end of this month. I've put in for Marine Barracks at Treasure Island, but I'll probably wind up at Pendleton. It sure would have been nice to get stationed close to home.

The holidays are coming and I pray that they bring many happy memories for our family and friends.

"80 days left"

Love Mike

JEFF LIPPKA, MEDIC—FEBRUARY 10TH, 2024

Courtesy of Jeff Lipka

My name is Jeff Lippka. I was a hospital corpsman in Echo, 2/1/1 in 1968. I can't recall when I first met Sgt. Gordon, but my first memory of him was during Operation Pegasus, which kicked off on April 1, 1968, from Ca Lu Valley. Sgt. Gordon, an E-5 sergeant, was our platoon commander after we lost our E-6 (staff sergeant). Platoon commanders were typically commissioned officers—first lieutenants. Sgt. Gordon was an excellent leader and well respected.

Toward the end of Pegasus, we were moving up a very steep hill in the heat of the day. The hill was thick with elephant grass that reached over our heads. We were told we had to get up the hill quickly. Although Sgt. Gordon kept us all moving, we had to rotate point men as they wore out. As the "doc," I tried to get him to stop or slow down, but to no avail. He did offer to carry some of my gear if I needed help. I didn't.

A few days later we were strung out along a ridge overlooking Highway 1 that led to Khe Sanh. The rumor was that our orders were to relieve the 27th that had been battling Viet Cong for 77 straight days. The expression of the day was: as a civilian, what's the worst they can do? Draft me. After being drafted, it was what's the worst they can do? Send me to Vietnam. Once in Vietnam, what's the worst they can do? I found out. We were sent out without our flak jackets because they would've been too hot to wear while humping the hills on Operation Pegasus. So, they did the worst to us —sent us to Khe Sanh without our flak jackets.

The choppers dropped us on the outskirts of the fire base, and we immediately began taking incoming fire. We scrambled to nearby trenches with the local Marines. After the incoming fire slowed down and stopped, we mounted up and headed in a staggered column into the fire base looking for our new home.

It was a relatively short way, but we once again began taking incoming rockets. It was every man for himself. After hitting the dirt, I spotted a gully nearby, scrambled over and dropped into a deep sloping trench where a truck was parked. The top was below ground level.

I felt fairly safe until there was another explosion nearby and a large chunk of shrapnel hit the hood of the truck I was crouched next to. Then I smelled fuel and realized that I was sitting next to a fuel truck. If it took a direct hit, there wouldn't be enough of me to scrape together to send home. I got the hell out of there fast.

Shortly after that, I learned that there had been other casualties nearby. I ran toward them and discovered that Sgt. Gordon and his radio man and the 81mm mortars radio man had all been hit. One of the radio men died. Not sure what happened to the other one; but I did see Sgt. Gordon briefly as they bandaged up a significant wound in his thigh. He looked ashen. It was very demoralizing to see our fearless leader like that. He was medevaced and I never saw him again. We heard he'd been further evacuated out of the country. For all these years I have been wondering what happened to him.

Sincerely,
Jeff Lippka

```
448P PST NOV 29 68 LC080
SYB502 SY WA435 XV GOVT PDB 2 EXTRA WASHINGTON DC 29 NFT
MR AND MRS JOHN WILLIAM GORDON, DONT PHONE, CHECK DLY CHGS
ABOVE 75 CTS
   6225 45ST SACRAMENTO CALIF THIS IS TO CONFIRM THAT YOUR SON
STAFF SERGEANT MICHAEL J GORDON USMC WAS INJURED 24 NOVEMBER
1968 IN QUANG NAM PROVINCE, REPUBLIC OF VIETNAM. HE SUSTAINED
FRAGMENTATION WOUNDS TO THE LEFT THIGH AND LEFT ARM FROM A
HOSTILE EXPLOSIVE DEVICE WHILE ON A PATROL. HE IS PRESENTLY
RECEIVING TREATMENT AT THE STATION HOSPITAL, DANANG. HIS CONDITION
AND PROGNOSIS WERE GOOD. YOUR ANXIETY IS REALIZED AND YOU ARE
ASSURED THAT HE IS RECEIVING THE BEST OF CARE. IT IS HOPED
THAT HE WILL COMMUNICATE WITH YOU SOON INFORMING YOU OF HIS
WELFARE. HIS MAILING ADDRESS REMAINS THE SAME. HIS BROTHERS
HAVE BEEN NOTIFIED
SF1201(R)LEONARD F CHAPMAN JR GENERAL USMC COMMANDANT OF THE MARINE
```

The notification of Michael's injury dated November 29th, 1968.

VIETNAM—NOVEMBER 26TH, 1968

Dear Dad & Mom,

Well by now you probably know I'm in the hospital again, but they still haven't got me yet. I'll be as good as new in a few weeks and because it is my second 48 hr Purple Heart[31] I'll be leaving Vietnam for good. In fact, if I'm lucky I may make it for Christmas.

I stepped in a booby trap and caught some fragments in my left leg and left arm. Sorry for the handwriting, but I am lying on my back writing this letter.

I'll write again soon.

                 Love Mike

---

31 The Purple Heart is awarded to service members who are wounded or killed in action that leads a medical officer to determine they are "not fit for full duty" for over forty-eight hours.

VIETNAM—NOVEMBER 27TH, 1968

Dear Dad and Mom,

Sorry for the short letter before, but I wanted you to know that I was alright and still in good shape. I still don't know what they're going to do with me, but one thing's for sure, I'm out of the combat zone for good. I'll probably wind up in Okinawa till my rotation date in February. I still haven't discounted the idea of being stationed in the hospital in the states till I'm fit for full duty again.

The booby trap that I stepped on was more concussion that anything else. It was nicely concealed though. I'm pretty good at spotting them, but I let up my guard at the wrong time. The Doctor sewed up my holes today so it won't be long till I'm as good as new!

Say hello to the family for me, and tell Johnny I haven't forgotten his present. I'll write again soon.

Love Mike

NAVY COMMENDATION MEDAL WITH COMBAT "V"—MARCH 8TH, 1969

The Secretary of the Navy takes pleasure in presenting the NAVY COMMENDATION MEDAL to

STAFF SERGEANT MICHAEL J. GORDON

UNITED STATES MARINE CORPS

for service as set forth in the following

CITATION:

"For meritorious service while serving as a Platoon Sergeant with Company E, Second Battalion, First Marines, First Marine Division in connection with operations against the enemy in the Republic of Vietnam from 10 January to 10 December 1968. Throughout this period, Staff Sergeant Gordon performed his demanding duties in an exemplary and highly professional manner. Constantly concerned for the combat readiness of his unit, he tirelessly trained and molded his men into an effective fighting force. Participating in seven major combat operations, including Operations Pegasus, Kentucky, and Scotland II, he displayed a superior knowledge of tactics as he aggressively led his men against the enemy on numerous occasions. On 22 November 1968, while maneuvering his platoon across an open rice paddy, his point element came under intense small arms fire from a well-entrenched hostile force. Rapidly assessing the situation, Staff Sergeant Gordon directed his men in returning a heavy volume of suppressive fire and then slowly withdrew his squads to a more tenable position from which he directed effective 81mm mortar fire on the enemy emplacements. His superb resourcefulness and exceptional initiative earned the respect and admiration of all who served with him and contributed significantly to the accomplishment of his unit's mission. By his leadership, professional competence and steadfast devotion to duty, Staff Sergeant Gordon upheld the finest traditions of the Marine Corps and of the United States Naval Service."

Staff Sergeant Gordon is authorized to wear the Combat "V".

FOR THE SECRETARY OF THE NAVY,

H. W. BUSE, JR.
LIEUTENANT GENERAL, U. S. MARINE CORPS
COMMANDING GENERAL, FLEET MARINE FORCE, PACIFIC

AFTERWORD

In that same gun safe containing the letters and medals of my dad's, there was one letter from my dad's father who had served on the USS *Colorado* a few years before Pearl Harbor. Cpl. John W. Gordon was writing to his own dad. His letter revealed my grandfather's yearning to know his dad, who'd been out of his life for years. This yearning would become generational among Gordon men.

Both my father and his father were looking for connection with fathers who broke or didn't keep those connections. I never knew my great granddad, only that his name was L.A. Gordon and that he lived in Oklahoma. Father-son ties have been brittle in my family and marked by anger and an unwillingness to forgive as emotional scars run deep. Despite my father's letters, the two men later broke ties after my dad returned home from the war. At some point they never spoke, and my grandfather wasn't welcome in our home. The same pattern of abandonment occurred between my grandfather and his dad, a sorrowful legacy that my father, thankfully, overcame.

When my father, Michael Gordon, returned home, he married his girlfriend, Kathie Evans, and had me and my two brothers, Chad and Robb. He became a successful businessman. He moved the family to Oregon, eventually founding his own business. He was a personable guy, which made him good at sales, and he was also adept at repairing, building and constructing just about anything he put his mind to.

My father carried many demons brought about by events from his own childhood, his relationship with his father, and the war. I am grateful for the good father that he was. He was a better man than his own father. In honor of my dad, I have strived to be a good man and a better father to my own two sons. I hope that I have made him proud.

The letter from my grandfather to his father shows the longing for family and father-son bonding:

USS *COLORADO*—OCTOBER 31ST, 1939

Dear Daddy,

I was so happy when I received your letter this morning. I think that it has been almost 10 years since I heard from you. But anyway, I was really glad to hear from my father and hear your side of the story. Mother told me her side of why you went away and didn't come back. But now that I read how you felt about it and I can see that you must have suffered a great deal.

I know that Mother was getting your letters and writing to you after it was already done. She could see how she was a bit too hasty in making her decision and wanted you back again. But she should have known better than to try to rekindle an old flame after she had already drowned it out by pouring water on it.

I love my Mother and always will, but I have always wanted to see my father too and now that I have definitely established correspondence with you, I don't think it will be long now before I will be able to come and see you.

I am terribly sorry that things had to happen like they did and there isn't anything in the world that I would rather have than my real Mother and Father. But Daddy it is all over now and we might just as well forget about it and make the best of it.

I think that you are the best Daddy in the world and I am just as proud of you as any son could be. I think that you did the right thing although it made it a little tough on all persons concerned.

It wasn't very pleasant living with a stepdad at times, but I tried to make the best of it and when I got big enough to stick up for myself I told him where to head in and we went round and round. But now I am big enough so I don't need to take much lip from anybody.

I have tried to be a good son and grow up so some day I could find my Father and he would be proud of his only son.

I haven't been an angel but I haven't done anything that I am ashamed of either. I am almost twenty-four and not ready to settle down yet.

Well Daddy it is almost nine p.m. and I was up on watch last night. I better hit the hay and get some shut eye.

Your loving son,
Johnny

www.ingramcontent.com/pod-product-compliance
Lightning Source LLC
LaVergne TN
LVHW061630070526
838199LV00071B/6636